Praise for *Relational Reset*

Relational Reset is such a sound, practical book. If you're struggling in your relationships to tell the truth or create good boundaries, or if you battle unmet expectations, you will find solace, wisdom, and biblical advice in the pages of this helpful resource.

MARY DEMUTH
Author of *The Seven Deadly Friendships: How to Heal When Painful Relationships Eat Away at Your Joy*

Do you find yourself easily offended, fearful, disappointed, or envious? If you need a grace-and-truth-filled emotional makeover, Dr. Laurel is in! Her conversational style is winsome and her words are wise. Apply this book to your life and find out for yourself that positive change is possible, even in your most challenging relationships.

ARLENE PELLICANE
Speaker and author of *Calm, Cool, and Connected: 5 Digital Habits for a More Balanced Life*

D1414818

Relational Reset

Unlearning the Habits That Hold You Back

DR. LAUREL SHALER

MOODY PUBLISHERS

CHICAGO

All Scripture quotations, unless otherwise indicated, are taken from the Holy Bible, New International Version®, NIV®. Copyright © 1973, 1978, 1984, 2011 by Biblica, Inc.™ Used by permission of Zondervan. All rights reserved worldwide. www.zondervan.com. The "NIV" and "New International Version" are trademarks registered in the United States Patent and Trademark Office by Biblica, Inc.™

Scripture quotations marked NLT are taken from the Holy Bible, New Living Translation, copyright © 1996, 2004, 2007 by Tyndale House Foundation. Used by permission of Tyndale House Publishers, Inc., Carol Stream, Illinois 60188. All rights reserved.

Scripture quotations marked AMPC are taken from the Amplified® Bible (AMPC), Copyright © 1954, 1958, 1962, 1964, 1965, 1987 by The Lockman Foundation. Used by permission. www.Lockman.org.

All italics shown in Scripture quotations have been placed by the author for emphasis.

Edited by Amanda Cleary Eastep
Author photo: Ashley Lawton
Interior design: Ragont Design
Cover design: Stephen Vosloo
Cover illustration of refresh icon copyright (c) 2018 by blankstock / Adobe Stock (165541068). All rights reserved.

Published in association with the literary agency of the Hartline Literary Agency, 123 Queenston Drive, Pittsburg, PA 15235.

All websites and phone numbers listed herein are accurate at the time of publication but may change in the future or cease to exist. The listing of website references and resources does not imply publisher endorsement of the site's entire contents. Groups and organizations are listed for informational purposes, and listing does not imply publisher endorsement of their activities.

This book is not intended to replace a one-on-one relationship with a qualified health care professional, but as a sharing of knowledge and information from the research and experience of the author. You are advised and encouraged to consult with your health care professional in all matters relating to your health and the health of your family. The publisher and author disclaim any liability arising directly or indirectly from the use of this book.

Names and details of some stories have been changed to protect the privacy of individuals.

Library of Congress Cataloging-in-Publication Data

Names: Shaler, Laurel, author.
Title: Relational reset : unlearning the habits that hold you back / Dr. Laurel Shaler.
Description: Chicago : Moody Publishers, 2019. | Includes bibliographical references.
Identifiers: LCCN 2018042643 (print) | LCCN 2018056250 (ebook) | ISBN 9780802497475 (ebook) | ISBN 9780802418722
Subjects: LCSH: Interpersonal relations--Religious aspects--Christianity. | Habit-breaking--Religious aspects--Christianity.
Classification: LCC BV4597.52 (ebook) | LCC BV4597.52 .S535 2019 (print) | DDC 248.4--dc23
LC record available at https://lccn.loc.gov/2018042643

We hope you enjoy this book from Moody Publishers. Our goal is to provide high-quality, thought-provoking books and products that connect truth to your real needs and challenges. For more information on other books and products written and produced from a biblical perspective, go to www.moodypublishers.com or write to:

Moody Publishers
820 N. LaSalle Boulevard
Chicago, IL 60610

1 3 5 7 9 10 8 6 4 2

Printed in the United States of America

To my loving husband, Nick.
Marriage is a beautiful symbol
of the relationship between Jesus Christ,
the Groom, and His Church, the bride. Thank you,
Nick, for modeling this relationship so well.
Our wedding verse becomes truer every day:
And the two will become one flesh.
Ephesians 5:31
Words cannot describe how much I love you.

And to our precious daughter, Anna Jean.
You are fearfully and wonderfully made, dear child.
May your relationship with God
be the one you pursue most of all.
But know too how much your mama loves you.
I'll never get over my thankfulness to God for
His indescribable gift. You, my daughter.

Contents

Introduction

Your basic need in life is for relationship.
HENRY CLOUD and JOHN TOWNSEND

As you're walking down the hallway at work, your coworker and friend idles past you. Instead of greeting you or even looking at you, she keeps her eyes laser-focused forward. You look tentatively at her, but don't make a sound because it's obvious she is ignoring you. You sigh and think: *What is her problem?* You run through just about all the possible explanations, becoming more insecure and defensive as the day passes. You decide if she is going to snub you, you are going to snub her right back.

You crawl into bed exhausted after another long and busy day. Your best friend has you all upset. Her comment at lunch that you could lose weight if you really tried hurt your feelings. You were so surprised by her words that you reacted harshly, retorting that the same was true for her. The two of you pushed food around your plates for a few more minutes in silence before quickly saying your goodbyes and heading off in opposite directions. You're still hurt by her comment, but also feeling guilty for your response. You cry as you lament that you just don't know what to do to repair the relationship. You want to apologize, but think, *She started it. She should apologize first.*

———————◆———————

It seems you and your husband aren't able to communicate without raising your voices at one another and bringing up the past. "Not this again," he says. "Can't you let it go? I've already apologized. When are you going to forgive me?" The problem is you don't know how to forgive, how to let it go. He's sick of being blamed for everything because of his past failures, and you are tired of being disappointed by him and living in fear that he'll leave you.

———————◆———————

If you see yourself and your relationships reflected in any of these scenarios . . . if you have one strained or several broken relationships . . . if you are tired of struggling because of your relationships, this book is for you!

Each chapter addresses a particular topic that hinders our ability to enjoy healthy relationships—with our spouses, parents, children, relatives, colleagues, friends, neighbors . . . really, anyone. You'll notice throughout how interconnected these issues are. We'll start by addressing insecurity, a struggle that impacts countless women in many ways. It leads us to become easily offended, jealous, judgmental, and afraid of rejection and abandonment, all of which we'll cover.

Perhaps disappointment seems like a constant companion. Or maybe you're haunted by past letdowns and afraid others will repeat the same offenses. Is your past holding you hostage, keeping you from having healthy relationships in the present as a result? Do you struggle to communicate how you are feeling? Perhaps every time you try, it seems things don't go well: you are misunderstood, you go into attack mode, you shut down, or you get defensive. In the pages that follow, we'll address all of these issues.

Be assured that it is possible to unlearn the bad habits that have damaged your relationships and to learn, instead, to respond to others in ways that will foster strong bonds. Rather than running to hide if someone is angry with you, you can learn to be the one to bridge the gap. Instead of wanting revenge when someone hurts or disappoints you, you can learn to leave that up to God and to forgive. Instead of waiting around for the other person to apologize, make amends, or reach out and repair the damage, you can learn to make the first move to restore a breakdown, to be the bigger person. You can learn to express your frustrations and fears, needs and wants, and love and commitment to others in a way that does not ruffle feathers, trigger defensiveness, or scream "I'm needy!"

When we develop empathy for others, act from realistic expectations, and take responsibility for our own thoughts, feelings, and behaviors, we gain freedom from the negativity that weighs us down and holds us back. When we toss off the weight of unhealthy patterns, we experience renewed strength and confidence . . . and a restored ability to move forward in our relationship with God and our relationships with others. As a counselor and a professor of counselor education and family studies, I wrote *Relational Reset: Unlearning the Habits That Hold You Back* to help you do just that.

My prayer for you is that this book will equip you to reclaim what God intended all along: healthy, whole, nurturing, loving, satisfying relationships. This can happen regardless of your past and within the many types of relationships in your life. Just think of the freedom you will feel and how much better you'll sleep when you aren't staying awake worrying about relationships. Even when others won't participate in improving a messy relationship, you can learn to be your best you and feel better for having done so.

If you're ready to take these steps, let's get started resetting our relationships together.

Silence Insecurity

B efore I met my husband, I was a part of a small group of singles and couples that spent a lot of time together. We enjoyed all the usual activities, such as trying new restaurants and hunting for good bargains, but usually we just liked hanging out. One night we were sitting in camp chairs around a fire, roasting marshmallows. We took turns using old coat hangers we'd fashioned into roasting sticks, dipping the marshmallows into the flames and pulling them out once they were black on the outside and gooey on the inside.

We were finishing our sugary treats as the coals were cooling off and the area was now only dimly lit. Ava, an introverted, beloved member of our gang, had been unusually quiet. Although she was sitting right next to me, I could barely see her brown eyes as she whispered the question that had been plaguing her all night:

"Are you mad at me?"

"No, Ava, I'm not mad at you," I softly replied.

"Are you sure you're not mad at me?" Ava asked a bit more boldly, wanting to be sure there was no conflict between us.

By this point, her boyfriend, who was sitting on her other side, leaned in to the conversation. Before I could respond to her question, he piped in.

"Ava," he said, "you've got to stop asking that all the time. If someone is upset with you, they'll tell you." He sighed and sat back in his chair, clearly frustrated—it wasn't the first time they'd had this conversation. To be honest, it wasn't the first time Ava and I had this conversation either.

A number of years after this marshmallow campout, I caught sight of a book on Ava's coffee table. It was called *So Long, Insecurity: You've Been a Bad Friend to Us.*[1] It had just been released, and Ava, recognizing her struggle, had read it right away. I casually asked about it, mentioning that maybe I should read it too. After she gushed about how much it had helped her personally, I replied a bit defensively, "Oh, I don't struggle with insecurity, but some of the clients that see me for therapy do. I'm sure there are some nuggets of wisdom I could share with them. Do you mind if I borrow it?"

I wasn't intentionally being deceptive. I just didn't realize at the time the role insecurity played in my life. I've always tried to put on a tough exterior, never wanting anyone to see my weaknesses or vulnerabilities. As a result, some of my relationships haven't been as real or deep as they could be, and, really, as they should be.

HOW SECURE ARE YOU?

What about you? Do you struggle with insecurity? If you aren't sure, let me ask you some questions. Have you ever picked up your cellphone over and over (and over and over) to see if someone has replied to your text or email, only to grow more and more anxious until you get the reply that everything's okay? Have you ever felt the need (without cause or justification) to check your boyfriend's or husband's cellphone history? Have you ever found yourself over-communicating "just to clarify"? If you answered yes to any of these, you may be struggling with insecurity.

Perhaps you find yourself feeling like you're not worthy of *something* in your relationships—of love, of attention, of time together, of forgiveness. Don't feel good enough? Smart enough? Attractive enough? That's insecurity.

Perhaps there's a negative voice from your past that you keep hearing in your mind, like a song on repeat. (*You talk too much. You are just too sensitive! Are you sure you can handle that?*) Except the voice in your head is so much worse than the current pop song you heard in the waiting room at the doctor's office.

Maybe the negative voice you're hearing is your own. (*How could I have messed up again? What is wrong with me? I'm so stupid.*) There might even be someone presently in your life triggering self-defeating thoughts and feelings through his or her words or actions. It could be that this individual doesn't even know how he or she is impacting you. In fact, that person may be insecure too.

Perhaps you recognize a friend or family member in these descriptions. The above behaviors are not the actions of people who feel secure, and relationships that involve an insecure party cannot remain unscathed for long. Sooner or later (perhaps even now), you or your loved one's insecurity is going to catch up with you. Like it did with Ava's boyfriend, the constant neediness will get old and frustrating. Few people have the energy or time to constantly reassure someone that the relationship is on solid ground.

Sometimes we bottle up the insecurity, never verbally expressing it, yet it seeps out anyway through our behaviors. For example, a 2014 *Glamour* survey found that over half of women who participated felt insecure about their bodies.[2] Can you relate? Are you the wife, mama, or friend who refuses to wear a swimsuit—always sitting on the sideline while everyone else splashes and plays in the pool or ocean? Or maybe you do put one on, but you're constantly trying to cover yourself up or running to the ladies' room to see how you look, resulting in less time with your family or friends. Perhaps you're constantly asking for reassurance from your husband or sister or kids that you look fine. Whether you express your insecurity through your words or through your behavior, you can be sure it's not helping you form strong bonds in your relationships.

The reality is this: *Everyone is insecure about something.* (As hard as this is to admit, "everyone" includes me.) Insecurity drives many of the issues we're going to explore in this book, such as envy and blame. Insecurity can also lead to fear of abandonment. This was the case for Ava.

For her, insecurity was like a self-fulfilling prophecy. Ava had so many doubts about herself that she believed that if she did anything wrong, a friend would stop talking to her or a boyfriend would break up with her. Her insecurity led to her constantly "checking in" to make sure there was no problem. Unfortunately, some of the folks she kept asking grew weary of her neediness, and as a result, her worst fear would come true. But it didn't have to be that way for Ava—and it doesn't have to be that way for you either.

The good news is this: *You can silence the insecurity.* It may not be possible 100 percent of the time, because so often we get in our own way. But we can definitely get a better handle on this issue that's been ailing us. It's time to evict the critics that have lived far too long in our own minds—those shaming, negative voices that weigh us down, leaving us distracted from what really matters. We—you—can break the chains of insecurity and be set free from this burden. The process of resetting relationships takes time and effort, but it's Oh. So. Worth. It.

As for me? Well, I went out and bought a copy of *So Long, Insecurity* for myself. Not only did I read it, I refer to it often. In fact, it's lying open right next to me as I write this first chapter. You see, we can't reset relationships without facing the insecurities that prevent us from thriving in our connections with other people.

In the following section we'll explore three things you can do to develop a more secure self, thus lessening the negative impact that insecurity has on your relationships.

STEPS TO SILENCING INSECURITY

If you Google the terms *self-esteem* and *self-worth*, you'll find many definitions for each. Some people will claim these are synonyms, but I disagree. Merriam-Webster states that self-esteem is "a confidence and satisfaction in oneself." Self-esteem can be fleeting and change at the drop of a hat. My own decreases if I'm having a bad hair day or decide that I don't like my outfit once I leave the house. If someone compliments something I've done, said, or written, I feel good about myself. If I write an article or blog that I believe is on a critical and timely topic, and it doesn't get many views or comments, I start to doubt myself. My confidence drops. Levels of self-esteem can fluctuate, sometimes simply based on how well you've slept or whether you're feeling bloated. (Am I right, friends?)

On the other hand, self-worth is how you look at yourself as a person, how you see your value as a human being.[3] Self-worth is about who you are at the *core*, and most importantly, *Whose* you are. In other words, it's all about knowing your place in Christ— and believing that you were created by God, in His image, and you are on this earth for a reason. As a mental health professional, but most importantly as a Christian, I believe having self-worth is far more important than having self-esteem.

Cultivate Self-Worth

Our self-worth is developed deep down inside of us, in our hearts and souls. It's how we identify ourselves at the core of who we are. Good self-esteem and low self-esteem come and go, while self-worth is long-term. Think of it this way: self-esteem is like the weather, which can fluctuate over a short period of time, while self-worth is like the climate, which follows a particular pattern over a long period of time. While the weather changes frequently, it does not change the climate. Likewise, our self-esteem ebbs and flows based on whatever is going on that day (or that minute), while our self-worth is who we believe ourselves to be at the center of our very being, regardless of what's going on around us. The good news is that if you have low self-worth, it can be improved!

So, how do self-esteem and self-worth play into relationships? Think about how you are in your most important relationships. What determines your mood? Your thoughts? Your behavior? Do you rely on things that change quickly, like the weather in the South? (One January day we had sunshine and 80s and then the next day, several inches of snow. Talk about temperamental!) Is how you view yourself dependent upon another person's actions? Or, do you choose your attitude and actions based on things that don't change—on who you are deep down, on your self-worth?

Oftentimes, what is going on in our relationships impacts how we view ourselves, and how we view ourselves impacts our relationships. Here's a case in point. Joan's thoughts about herself are based on her relationship with her husband. When he is considerate and kind toward her, doing things like cleaning up the kitchen or bringing her flowers for no reason, her self-esteem improves. But when he slacks off in communicating with her in a way that demonstrates his love for her, she starts to think she must not be worth it. She sinks into a dark hole of believing her husband doesn't love her. In turn, she grows insecure in the relationship, snapping at him and questioning him.

However, instead of falling into this cycle like a hamster on a wheel, Joan could choose to remind herself that who she is does not change based on her husband's—or anyone's—behavior toward her. Her core being is still the same; she is not less desirable or less lovable simply because her husband hasn't been helping around the house as much. While *that* is a different issue to address, it doesn't have to trigger her to feel insecure about her worth, and, as a result, insecure about the marriage either.

[If you know your worth in Christ, even when you have good relationship days and bad relationship days, you can come back to our true identity.] You can feel good about who we are if we are living to please the audience of the One who really matters. Your self-worth, thoughts, and actions . . . they all have to come back to God, or you may experience an emotional self-esteem roller coaster that puts the worst case of PMS you've ever seen to shame. [Your identity in Christ can be an anchor in the midst of the ups and downs of your earthly relationships. Just because a friend doesn't get back to you doesn't mean you're a failure at friendship. Having a spat with your spouse doesn't make you a wretched wife. In other words, you don't have to feel insecure about relationships *just because they're not perfect*. And just because you're not perfect doesn't mean your self-worth has to suffer.]

Another way of overcoming insecurity and cultivating self-worth is through biblical affirmations. We'll take a look at those next.

Remind Yourself of Whose You Are

Leigh was always on the move, and my motto with her was: "If you're driving, I'm riding." It was fun to get on the road with her and set out on an adventure. When we lived in the same small town, we took many fun drives toward whatever "big city" destination she had chosen for that day. On one occasion, she turned on a CD that contained self-affirmations. Before we actually got to those, we had to go through some put-you-to-sleep instructions about the affirmations. A couple of times we accidentally missed the beginning of the affirmations (because it's hard to hear over the sound of the GPS telling you to turn left in five million feet). After rewinding the CD a couple of times, Leigh asked me, "Do you want me to rewind it again?" Before I could stop myself, I shouted "No!" after which we fell into peals of laughter.

After we finally got through the Top 50 affirmations (yes—50!),

Leigh asked me what my favorite was. Hmm. Which one should I go with? Maybe "I love listening to my affirmation CD" (no self-indulgent plug there) or "I like to smile" (huh?). That conversation kept us laughing.

But, then, it was time to get serious. I told Leigh that while I believe in self-talk and use the technique frequently, I have found what I believe to be a better way. That better way is the truth found in God's Word. As a believer, I feel much better about *who* I am when I remind myself *Whose* I am. I remind myself that God loves me and that being in relationship with Him means I have access to Him through prayer and His Word, the Bible, as my guide. Repeating scriptural truths that tell you who you are and Whose you are can do a world of good.

I'll list some of my favorites to get you thinking in that direction:

- "If God is for [me], who can be against [me]?" (Rom. 8:31)
- "I am fearfully and wonderfully made." (Ps. 139:14)
- "But by the grace of God I am what I am." (1 Cor. 15:10)
- "We have been made holy through the sacrifice of the body of Jesus Christ once for all." (Heb. 10:10)
- "See what great love the Father has lavished on us, that we should be called children of God! And that is what we are!" (1 John 3:1)

I encourage you to create your own list of biblical affirmations. You can commit them to memory and even record them, reminding yourself over and over of your place as a princess, a daughter of the King. (I don't even think I would mind rewinding these affirmations over and over!)

The next time you are feeling insecure in a relationship—or even before—and you're starting to question everything ("She's mad at me," "He doesn't like me anymore," "My boss doesn't think I can do anything right"), try repeating these verses.

Yes, repeating biblical affirmations over and over to yourself is self-talk. But, it is not selfish talk. Satan will use any tactic he can to get to you—as the father of lies, he will surely lie. And he will use those lies to trigger insecurity in you. But when you repeat God's Word over and over, you are affirming truths that calm your heart and soothe your soul, reminding you that God is for you and that you are fearfully and wonderfully made. You are who you are by His grace! You are holy; you are loved; you are a child of God. That is who you are. God's is Whose you are!

It's His praise you should be seeking, not the praise of those with whom you're in relationship. After all, we're all just human. Let's take a look at one more step in overcoming insecurity.

Seek God's Praise Alone

John 12:42–43 says this: "Yet at the same time many even among the leaders believed in him. But because of the Pharisees they would not openly acknowledge their faith for fear they would be put out of the synagogue; for they loved human praise more than praise from God." The Scriptures could not be more clear: these people "loved human praise more than praise from God." Sadly, because of their fear, they chose not to acknowledge their faith. They were so concerned about what other people would think about them, and what other people would do to them, that they chose to please people over God.

Keep in mind that these folks had seen Jesus face to face. Jesus had just ridden into Jerusalem through these crowds of people who were shouting "Hosanna!", "Blessed is he who comes in the name of the Lord!", and "Blessed is the King of Israel!" He had even predicted His death, and while many still did not believe in Him, many *did* believe (see John 12:42). They had seen the miracles He performed. They'd heard His words. They *believed*. Yet, they still would not publicly acknowledge their faith in Him.

While the Pharisees generally deserve the bad rap they get, I can't help but think I am often no better than they. For example, before posting a message on social media, I often find myself wondering what people will think more than I consider what God will think—*Who will be offended by this?* rather than, *Is this true to the Bible and honoring to God?*

It's easy to fall into the trap of doing what others desire of us rather than what God demands. This is particularly true when we are insecure in our relationships. In Galatians 1:10, Paul writes, "Am I now trying to win the approval of human beings, or of God? Or am I trying to please people?" Notice how he emphasizes the question by asking it twice. *Who am I trying to please?* Maybe I want my boss to notice me so I get the promotion (or at least keep my job), so I agree to doing something I know is unethical. Perhaps I don't want to lose a friend, so I verbally agree with her on everything, even when I don't agree in my heart. To be concerned about careers, friendships, or *anything* more than God is to replace God with an idol. And it does nothing for relationships, because people-pleasing simply can't ease insecurity.

Why do we care more about what other people think than what God thinks? Why would we want their praise over the praise of the Creator of the universe? *Insecurity.*

I want to be in the business of pleasing God, and the only way to do that is to place my security in Him alone. By doing so, I can be in a right relationship with Him as I work on resetting relationships with others so that they become more like what He created them to be.

NO MORE INSECURITY

Insecurity damages relationships, while being secure strengthens them. If I know my self-worth, and my identity in Christ, and seek His approval, then I will feel freer to be myself, to be honest, to set boundaries, to let go of envy and blame, and to use my relationships to glorify God rather than to satisfy myself.

Remember Ava? After many years of struggling, she sought help—both self-help and professional help—to wrangle this problem before it became worse. She had lost several friends and boyfriends and knew she had to do something different. While she didn't marry the guy at the s'more fest, she did eventually get married. He (and her friends) no longer hear, "Are you mad at me?" and "Is everything okay with us?" Ava is now secure enough in herself and in her relationships that she no longer feels compelled to obsessively wonder about and ask those questions. Instead, she knows her relationships are solid, and she is able to trust that if there is a problem, she will be the first to know. She is successfully doing the work to silence insecurity. You can too.

WORKING ON MYSELF

1. Has insecurity affected a relationship in your life? If so, how?

   _____

   _____

   _____

2. What have you done to silence your insecurity? Has this helped you? If so, how?

   _____

   _____

   _____

3. What does God's Word say about the security you can have in God?

_____

_____

_____

4. What biblical affirmations can you repeat to yourself when you are feeling insecure?

_____

_____

_____

Dear Lord,

Thank You for the promises I have in You. I know that in You, I can be totally secure. I can know my rightful place as a daughter of the King and rest in the assurance that I can live eternally with You because Jesus paid for my sins by dying on the cross. Please protect me from the lies of Satan.

I know that my insecurities and the insecurities of others can bring about conflict in relationships. I don't want that to happen. Help me be more secure and help my loved ones be more secure. Help me live my life as a model of someone firmly rooted in Your foundation. Lord, help me be a light for others.

For it's in the name of Jesus I pray.

Amen.

Deal with Disappointment

Nancy and Sara never forgot each other's birthdays. Even after they were both married with kids of their own, living hundreds of miles apart and unable to spend hours on the phone catching up like they used to, they each made a point to contact one another at least one day a year. Snail mail birthday cards had been replaced by electronic social media greetings. Then one year on Sara's birthday, Nancy picked up her phone before she even got out of bed. She excitedly opened up Facebook, hoping to be among the first to post a celebratory message filled with emoticons of cake, balloons, and gifts. It only took a few moments for her to realize her longest-standing friend had unfriended her. Feeling confused and disappointed, she wondered what she'd done and why her friend had shut her out.

We all have disappointments, some small and some great, from the game being rained out to a failed adoption. Disappointments can start off like a snowball that rolls down a hill, gathering more and more snow until it becomes a snow "boulder."

Often, our disappointments are related to other people, and regardless of size, they can cause us a lot of heartache. Your child's father cancels another visitation, leaving you angry and your son disappointed. Your teenage daughter sneaks out of the house to meet up with a boy. Yeah, you're definitely not happy with her. Your friend cancels your lunch date for the third time in a row. How disappointing.

Sometimes our disappointment isn't caused by the other person, but by outside circumstances that can damage the relationship nonetheless. For instance, your husband loses his job. (*I know it's not his fault, but I'm so disappointed.*) Or maybe you receive a diagnosis of infertility. (*My husband is so upset. I am too. I know it's not my fault, but it feels like it is.*) Your sibling's child comes down with the flu and the family can't make it to your special event. (*Of course they should stay home, but I am so upset they won't be here for me.*) Although no one is at fault, you still feel disappointment.

Whether trivial or earth-shattering, disappointing events can have a tremendous impact on our emotional well-being and on our relationships. How we react to these blows not only affects the relationship we have with the one who failed us, but all of our other relationships. One person disappoints us, so we expect others to. Or, we can't move past the setback, and we anticipate that the same person will disappoint us repeatedly; we wind up feeling angry and anxious.

It's impossible to go through life without being disappointed. But how do we deal with that fact so that we and our relationships are emotionally healthy? This chapter will help answer that question as we explore how our expectations may be setting us up for disappointment, and what we can do to recognize our triggers and reset our responses.

Are Your Expectations Realistic?

You know the expression "to have a friend, you have to be a friend." While that is true, it's also important to remember that how you function as a friend may not be the way your friend functions because of his or her personality or personal limits. For example, you may think a "good" friend is someone you speak with face to face once a week, and so you expect that from your close friends. Yet, some of your friends may not be able to meet with you once a week. You might be thinking, *Well, I work full time and have kids too, but I make the time. Why can't she make the time?* Regardless of what you think your friends should do, you need to be realistic about what you expect from them.

When it comes to having realistic expectations of others, I can think of no better role model than Jesus. He was no stranger to disappointment. Even His closest circle of friends, His disciples—family, really—did not always demonstrate belief or faith in Him.

The disciples fell asleep numerous times while Jesus prayed in the garden of Gethsemane despite being asked by Jesus to watch and pray. Three times Jesus asked, and three times His disciples failed Him.

Judas betrayed Him. Oh, how Judas betrayed Him.

Peter denied Him. Not once. Not twice. But three times. And this was after Jesus had told Peter that he would, and Peter said, "No way. Not me. Not ever." But he did.

Before they saw the risen Christ, many of the disciples abandoned Jesus by not even showing up for His crucifixion or burial. Who would have thought that Nicodemus, the man who would only come to Jesus at night, would have been the one to purchase seventy-five pounds of myrrh and spices in order to prepare the body of the Savior? Where were the disciples? We know John was there, but what about the others?

Thomas doubted Him. He saw the resurrected Jesus face to face, yet refused to believe He was really the Christ until he saw the nail marks in His hands and the wound in His side where He had been speared.

Jesus knew exactly what His disciples would do. He understood that they were human: therefore, sinners. He knew that because of sin, they would disappoint others, including Him. Not only did He know that the disciples would disappoint Him, He even knew what their actions would be long before they did. But Jesus never pulled back or tried to retaliate. He loved and accepted the disciples despite their hurtful actions toward Him. He accepted that they were merely human, and that they couldn't be perfect.

All of us can benefit from having this expectation: people will disappoint us. Friends will disappoint us. Family will disappoint us. Fellow church members, neighbors, employers, colleagues . . . they will all disappoint us. *We'll disappoint others too.* If we're not careful, we'll expect perfection from others. If so, when disappointment comes, it can crush us and our relationships. The Lord knows we don't want anyone expecting us to be perfect, so we shouldn't expect that from others either.

For example, do you have unrealistic expectations of your spouse? (*I'm frustrated that my husband is not as romantic as I had hoped he would be. Should I consider a separation?*) Do you have unrealistic expectations of your coworkers? (*If I can handle this big of a caseload without any problem, why can't she?*) Do you have unrealistic expectations of your pastor? (*He knows I'm homebound. Why can't he come to visit me every week?*) Are any of these questions hitting home? Then it's possible your expectations of others are too high.

Not long after the birth of my second nephew, my sister drove her two boys about an hour to my city to visit our mother in the hospital. Since the boys were too young to go in, I agreed (okay, asked) to watch them. We were having a Christmas dinner and program at my church that evening, and I thought it would be fun to have them along. My husband was working late, so I was solo with an almost three-year-old and a ten-week-old. The dinner was a balancing act—carrying the little one in his car seat while hanging on to the older one while loading up two plates of yummy foods and delicious desserts. (I'm Southern Baptist, after all.) I was barely managing it all by the time I made it to a table, set the baby carrier down, got my older nephew settled, and collapsed into my own chair. Thankfully, a sweet friend saw me and offered to help me for the rest of the night. But I learned a powerful lesson that evening—what it's like to wrangle kids. It was the first time I fully realized how hard it was, and I started to understand why some of my friends who had children were not as available as they once were.

Considering I was twenty-eight years old at the time, I was a little late to that knowledge. Nevertheless, it helped me to lower my expectations of others by recognizing that everyone is balancing something. It may not always be two kids and plates of food, but everyone has a lot going on in life. Our expectation that others ask "how high?" when we say "jump" (or any variation of this) can lead us down a rabbit hole that leads to disappointment.

I love the Golden Rule, which says, "Do to others as you would have them do to you" (Luke 6:31). I believe in that. I stand by that. And while I strive to always practice it, I don't succeed all the time. Neither does anyone else, and I have to be prepared for that. So do you. The reality is that not everyone will act how we want them to. Anytime we place people on a pedestal, they will fall. Ourselves included. We cannot hold people to the standard of perfection. But when people fail us—and they will—we can respond in ways that are good for our emotional well-being and can help us maintain healthy bonds with others. We'll look at one way to do this next.

REFRAMING AND REDEEMING THE DISAPPOINTMENT

Despite having graduated high school almost two decades ago— and going through several more schools and graduations since then—I can still vividly recall some disappointments I faced during those adolescent years.

When I was in the eleventh grade, I was not elected to a position

I really wanted for my senior year. I was so disappointed and didn't understand why I didn't get what I had worked three years for. I believed I would be the best fit for the position and deserved to be elected. Then, as the fall of my 12th grade year began, the grocery store I worked for was hosting a grocery-bagging contest. You've never heard of this? It's a high-stakes competition that involves customer-service skills, speed of bagging, grocery placement in the bags (is the bread on top of the eggs or being crushed under them?), and weight distribution of groceries. Much to my surprise, I won that contest . . . and went on to win three more to become the Grocery Bagging Champion. As a result, I won a college scholarship and a weeklong trip to San Francisco to compete in the national grocery bagging championship. I didn't win, but it was an incredible experience. One that I would not have had the time for had I won that election. Besides, many people get to be student body president, but who gets to travel across the country as a high school senior for such a unique competition? As a result, I was able to let go of not only my disappointment in not winning the high school election, but also my disappointment in the people I thought had let me down. God redeemed my disappointment!

Over and over again, God has redeemed my disappointments through the plans He has for me. I am reminded of Proverbs 16:9, "In their hearts humans plan their course, but the LORD establishes their steps." When I am tempted to be disappointed in people and things not going as I want them to, it's helpful to remember the past times that God has led me to something even greater.

While God doesn't always work in quite that way, He can always use our disappointment. He can turn our ashes to beauty (Isa. 61:3). He can even use disappointments in relationships to bring us closer to one another. Think of the times disappointment has led to a needed conversation that resulted in a closer connection. Remember Nancy and Sara? When Nancy realized that Sara had unfriended her, she didn't know what to make of it. *Did she do it on accident or on purpose? If it was intentional, why?* Nancy decided to test the waters by texting Sara "Happy Birthday." Sara replied to her birthday text with a "Thanks so much! Hope you are doing well!" Nancy was all the more confused, but decided she would wait until the next day before saying anything further. After all, it was still Sara's birthday. Nancy prayed about how to approach her friend. She didn't want to come off accusatory since she didn't really know what happened. Feeling too upset to call, Nancy decided to email.

> Dear Sara,
>
> I hope you had a wonderful birthday yesterday! I can't wait to hear all about it! Please let me know a good time to call. I also wanted to touch base with you about something else. When I went on Facebook yesterday to wish you a happy birthday, it appeared that we were no longer friends. I hate to ask, but did you happen to unfriend me? I know it could have been an accident, but I wanted to make sure we are okay. I know we aren't as close as we used to be, but our friendship means so much to me!
>
> Love, Nancy

Nancy waited anxiously for a reply, but didn't have to wait long before her phone rang. It was Sara. In their ensuing conversation, Sara apologized for not calling sooner. She explained that, yes, she had unfriended Nancy after becoming increasingly uncomfortable with Nancy's political posts. Sara never talked politics, and it was a surprise to Nancy to learn they were so different in this department. Yet, they both agreed that despite their differences, their friendship was worth preserving. As a result of their conversation, they felt like they knew each other better than they had in years, and they renewed their commitment to stay in touch more. On the phone!

The next time you are disappointed in someone (or if you are still lingering on a past hurt), attempt to reframe the experience in an honest way. In other words, don't twist it around or lie to yourself, but truly explore how God has or can redeem the hurt, how He can make it into something beautiful, how He can bring you closer together. Here are a few examples of what this might look like:

- Your husband loses his job, and you are disappointed in him. Look at this as an opportunity for him to secure a better position. Work together to explore potential jobs while also teaming up to tighten your budget.
- Your friend cancels your lunch date after you secured a babysitter. Consider eating at home and spending the lunch money on a relaxing pedicure—don't waste the babysitter!
- Your boss overlooked you for a promotion. Or, perhaps he demoted you. Consider the fact that fewer responsibilities means more time for the volunteer work you love.

YOU CAN THRIVE . . .

I am a card hoarder. Well, not really, but I do have ten boxes of cards and a stack of single cards within my eyesight as I type this. One card has been in my stack for years, but I have yet to give it to anyone. It reads:

A true friend is loving, dependable and caring, all the things you are . . . I hope one day I can be as good a friend to you as you have always been to me.

This card has made many moves with me. It's seen more homes than many people do in their lifetime. (Military and work has led my husband and me to four states, five apartments, and five houses, if I am doing the math correctly.) You may be wondering why I've never given this card to anyone. It's hard to admit, but in the past, my expectations of others were awfully high. Thankfully, as I have grown older, they have become more realistic. I can recognize amazing qualities in friends who may not have as much time for me as I'd like. I can still see them as loving, dependable, caring, and more. Nowadays I keep this card on my desk, not because I don't think my friends are deserving of it, but because it serves as a reminder to be realistic in my expectations so that I don't wind up unnecessarily disappointed.

Did you catch that I said "unnecessarily" disappointed? I did so because even if our expectations are realistic, we *will* experience disappointments in this life. And even after reframing them and seeing how God redeems them, you may still struggle with the emotional impact or feel disconnected from the person who disappointed you.

Throughout this book, you'll learn various techniques to help you improve your relationships. Many of these—such as setting boundaries and talking honestly with others—will aid you in dealing with the disappointments. In addition to learning how to reduce your emotional distress, you'll also learn how to build healthier bonds and thrive, both in relationship and as an individual.

WORKING ON MYSELF

1. Reflect on some of the disappointments you have had in your relationships. What role did your expectations play in your disappointment? List the expectation and how it led to disappointment.

   _____

   _____

   _____

2. Knowing what you now know, how would you adjust
   each of the expectations you mentioned above?

   _____

   _____

   _____

3. Think about a disappointment that is weighing on
   your mind. How can you reframe this in a way that is
   both truthful and helpful to you?

   _____

   _____

   _____

4. What disappointment have you experienced that God
   redeemed by taking you to something better than you
   had planned for yourself?

   _____

   _____

   _____

Dear Jesus,

*You know that I've had unrealistic expectations of people,
which has caused me to be unnecessarily disappointed. I've
also gone through disappointing experiences. Please help me
have reasonable expectations of others, and of myself, and
learn to reframe my disappointments . . . to see how You can
redeem them or turn my ashes into beauty. In Jesus' name.*

Amen.

3

Overcome Offenses

A new clothing company had just come out that utilized consultants to sell their trendy tees and luxurious leggings. Most
sales took place online, but I was hesitant to purchase without
trying on the clothes. Not knowing any local consultants, I reached
out to some friends. One happened to know a young woman who
set up shop in an RV outside her home, which she opened from
time to time. Customers could visit in person, look around, and
use the tiny makeshift dressing room to try on the tees, leggings,
skirts, and dresses.

When the day arrived for the next open shopping event, I
made my way up the windy mountain road to the woman's property. I was getting a bit nervous that this was nothing more than
a lure when I turned the corner and saw the RV parked beside a
house. I breathed a sigh of relief and pulled off to the side of the
road behind a van that was loaded down with a mom, dad, and
more than a few kiddos. The husband took the children down the
road a bit farther to play while the wife and I walked into the RV
together. In turn, we introduced ourselves to the consultant, who

asked what we were looking for. The woman I had walked in with peered out the window to make sure her family was out of earshot.

Her eyes lit up as she told us, "My husband promised me three new dresses in exchange for putting up with his mother for an entire week." But then she went on, "Let me tell you, it was tough! Everything she said the entire week just flew all over me." (The southern way of saying her mother-in-law was pushing all her buttons.)

She continued, "Nothing I do is ever good enough for her. I can't tell you the number of times she has hurt my feelings. My husband thinks I am being too sensitive. Either way, we're like Marie and Debra on *Everybody Loves Raymond*. I'm glad to be getting these three dresses, but I don't think spending a week with her was worth it."

As the consultant chuckled and nodded affirmatively, helping the woman sort through the rack of dresses, I casually looked through the clothing. While I slid one hanger at a time to the left in order to get a better view of the next piece, I felt grateful that I get along well with my mother-in-law. But then I thought, *We women get easily offended an awful lot.*

OH NO SHE DIDN'T

People use all kinds of expressions to describe being upset or offended. You've just read about the southern expression, "Flew all over me." Another common one is, "Well I never!" As if to say, "Well, I have never been so offended in my entire life!" A similar expression that comes to mind is, "Oh no she didn't." When I conducted a Google search to remind myself of the origins of this phrase, I couldn't find any solid answer, despite pages of references. No matter, here are some of the examples of how the expression is used when someone:

Takes credit for your big idea at work. *Oh no she didn't.*

Passes the buck (or blame) on to you. *Oh no she didn't.*

Gives you a backhanded compliment. (*Your hair looks so much better since you had it cut.*) *Oh. No. She. Didn't!*

From little offenses to major ones, it's easy to get upset—to get our feelings hurt—when someone has, or we perceive they have, done wrong to us. Regardless of whether we have cause to be offended, when we take offense, our relationship with the other person can suffer.

For example, Hannah and Samantha were thrilled to score jobs as colleagues for the same up-and-coming company. Recently, Hannah was surprised to learn that she had been left out of a budding leaders group that their boss had placed Samantha in charge of. Hannah was offended that she wasn't assigned to the group. She was embarrassed, and since she thought Samantha was the one who had left her out of the group, she was angry as well. Hannah told some coworkers that Samantha had cut her out on purpose, claiming that Samantha just didn't want to compete with her. As it turned out, Hannah *was* left out intentionally, but it was their boss who had given Samantha the instruction not to include Hannah.

When Hannah found out the back story of what had happened, it didn't undo the damage done when she took offense. She was embarrassed that their boss thought more highly of Samantha as a future leader *and* ashamed of herself for spreading rumors about her friend. Samantha was upset that Hannah had spoken ill of her around the office. As a result, neither felt comfortable around the other, and they started avoiding each other at work as much as possible. Their relationship outside the office had cooled off completely. In reflecting on this experience, Hannah wished she had gone straight to Samantha or their boss instead of telling coworkers that Samantha was out to get her. She realized she had been too easily offended.

As hard as it is to say (and I know it's tough to hear): perhaps you too are easily offended. (*Oh yes I did.*) It's easy to blame others when we get hurt, but the truth is, we are the ones who have control over our emotions. And we can choose whether to feel offended.

HOW EASY ARE YOU TO OFFEND?

The word *snowflake* has taken on a whole new meaning. It used to refer to the cold, white substance that fell from the sky. My husband knows all about it, being from Minnesota. Not so, where I'm from. At the first hint of snow, my South Carolina city shuts down, and all the bread and milk gets snatched up from the grocery store shelves. On the rare occasion (about once a year) that we do get the fluffy stuff, I love it—cozied up in a warm blanket lying on the couch in front of my fire while drinking hot chocolate and staring out the wall of windows in my den. It's peaceful and serene watching each snowflake fall.

"Snowflake" is also a word often used to refer to a person who thinks she is more special than anyone else and should be treated as such . . . a person who believes the world revolves around her and who becomes upset when, for whatever reason, it doesn't. Think for a moment about the people in your life. Can you picture anyone who appears to easily take offense? Do you? This is an important chapter, and one that may challenge you to reassess your responses to the words and actions of others.

Now, there may be a good reason or multiple reasons people may seem sensitive on occasion. You never know what circumstances someone is facing and why that person may react in a certain way. A recent breakup, a sobering health diagnosis, stress, or just not feeling well can all result in a person's feelings being hurt more easily and more often. In addition, certain past hurts or relationships that damaged self-esteem could cause someone to respond in ways that seem out of proportion with the perceived offense. For example, your friend perceives you are picking on her, and begins to yell at you. You respond with, "I'm just playing around," which leads her to storm off. You may not know that the extensive abuse she suffered at the hands of a parent was always excused with, "I'm just playing around."

At the same time, some people seem to take offense regularly and for myriad reasons. The term "snowflake" may quickly come to mind when you think of them. But how easily do you recognize that propensity in yourself? Consider, honestly, whether or not *you* are easily offended by answering the following questions:

- Do you find that your feelings are frequently hurt?
- Have people told you they feel as if they have to walk on egg-shells around you?
- Are you constantly feeling aggrieved?
- Do you frequently expect someone to apologize?
- Are you constantly repeating the words, "You hurt my feelings"?

If you answered yes to any of these questions, the issue probably isn't the number of offensive people around you. Could *you* possibly be the problem? If there's a chance you are too easily offended, let's look together at two ways you can lower your "offense-ometer."

Lowering Your Offense-Ometer

You have probably heard the terms *empathy* and *grace* before. You may have even tried to put them into practice. In this section, I want us to look at these concepts with a fresh perspective. Here, we'll see what it means to become empathetic and to extend grace toward those who have offended us.

When you develop empathy and respond to others with grace, you may find the needle on your offense-ometer declining, much like the speedometer on your car drops as you step on the brake before sailing through a red light. The yellow light was your warning, but if you see it too late or ignore it, you can face any number of consequences, from getting a ticket to getting in a car accident. But if you pay attention and heed the warning, you can avoid those kinds of results. In the case of relationships, the "yellow light" is your awareness that you are too easily offended. It's time to take action, before the light hits red. If you don't put the brakes on now, you will sail through that red light and may very well crash. So, be empathetic *now*. Extend grace *now*. These are qualities that contribute to our emotional well-being and increase our resistance to taking offense.

Develop Empathy Toward Those Who Hurt You

In my first book, *Reclaiming Sanity: Hope and Healing for Trauma, Stress, and Overwhelming Life Events*, I wrote about how to develop empathy for someone who has wronged you. Because empathy is such an effective way for us to overcome offenses, I want to highlight a few additional ideas here.

Empathy starts by putting yourself in the other person's shoes and trying to see things through that person's eyes. While you can't (and shouldn't) mind-read, you can imagine how that person may answer the following questions:

- What is it like to be this person? Try and think through what it would be like to be the person who offended you.

- Why might this person have treated you the way he or she did? This builds on the answers to the first question.

- How might this person want to be treated in return? I think the answer to this is obvious, but I'll say it anyway. She would want to be treated with grace. She would want to be met with mercy.

Here's an example of how we can put these questions to practical use:

Rosie was a young single mom who had recently moved next door to another young single mom. They hit it off as soon as they met due to all they had in common. They became fast friends and spent a lot of time together with their children. The neighbor sometimes asked Rosie for help, and Rosie was usually willing to do things like pick up extra milk while she was at the store or pick up the neighbor's kids when she picked up her own from school. Lately, however, the requests were more frequent and, worse, more demanding.

Let's listen in on a conversation they had, which triggered Rosie to feel offended:

Neighbor: "Rosie, would you swing by the library on the way home? John needs to pick up a book for a school report."

Rosie: "Honestly, I'm not feeling well today and was planning to come straight home with the kids."

Neighbor: "Well, he really needs the book today, and I don't have time to get there after work."

Rosie: "I'm sorry—I understand the predicament, but I just can't go today."

Neighbor: "Ugh. Thanks a lot, Rosie. I mean—I work full time and you stay home on disability. I don't understand why you can't do this one thing for me!"

I'm sure it's obvious *why* Rosie was offended. Her neighbor and friend seemed to take her acts of kindness for granted and acted as if Rosie should do whatever she asked, simply because Rosie did not work a full-time job. What she forgot was that Rosie was on disability for a reason. Many days, she was in too much pain to do much more than get her kids to and from school and make sure they had a decent supper. On good days, she did as much as possible to compensate for the bad days. Rosie was frustrated that her friend didn't acknowledge all she had done for her and was offended at the insinuation that she wasn't suffering and should do whatever she asked.

Now, let's take a look at how Rosie can develop empathy for her neighbor by reflecting on the three questions listed earlier.

What is it like to be this person? Rosie took some time to remember how difficult it is to be a single mom who also works full time. She had been there and done that before being involved in a serious car accident. So it was relatively easy for her to put herself in her friend's shoes. She recalled being exhausted at the end of a busy work day after having gotten up in the wee hours of the morning to feed, clothe, and drive the kids to school all by herself. When the clock struck 6:00 p.m., she was ready to go home too—just in time to make dinner, help the kids with homework, bathe them, tuck them in, and collapse into bed herself, just to start the whole routine again a few hours later. She knew it was tough to squeeze anything else into that schedule. She understood why her friend was asking for help. To be honest, she wished she had asked for more help herself.

This question was easy for Rosie to answer because she had been in similar circumstances as her neighbor. But even if you have not actually "been there," you can still put yourself in someone else's place. Envision the other person's life, both the present and the past that contributed to the present. You may not know all the details, but you may know enough to know that it would be stressful to be a boss or that it would be exhausting to be a new mom. You're not looking to excuse the behavior, but to understand the person's position better.

Why might this person have treated me the way he or she did? Rosie might be able to conclude something like this: "My neighbor is frustrated. She has very little time and is stretched. She looks at me not working and forgets it's because I'm disabled. We are both doing the best we can."

How might this person want to be treated in return? Rosie could treat her neighbor kindly while also remaining firm in her stance in an effort to preserve the relationship and maintain her necessary boundaries. For example, when her neighbor asked her to swing by the library on the way home, she could reply: "I enjoy helping you out when I can, because I know how hard you work. Before I was in my accident, I worked full time while raising my kids alone too, so I know what it's like. As you know, I now have to stay at home due to my disability, and some days are better than others. On good days, I am happy to help you out. On bad days, I'm really sorry, but I will need to rest. I hope you understand because I cherish our friendship."

Extend Grace

Much like forgiveness is a choice, not being easily offended is also a choice. Ecclesiastes 7:21–22 says: "Do not pay attention to every word people say, or you may hear your servant cursing you—for you know in your heart that many times you yourself have cursed others."

Two points we can take away from these verses are:

Don't look to be offended or else you'll find it. If you are
constantly listening in on what others are saying, then you
are likely to hear them say things about you that you don't
like—or you may just *think* they're talking about you. In
other words, if you are looking to be offended, you'll take
offense. If you think your friend has intentionally left you
out when she thanked all her "besties" on Facebook, guess
what? You are going to be offended! As you scroll through
your Facebook or Twitter feed, you just *know* your friend
is talking about your posts when she says she is "sick and
tired of seeing x, y, z on Facebook," and you get offended.

Or maybe you're walking past your coworker's closed
door, and you hear her talking to someone else in hushed
whispers. You decide she *must* be talking about you. You
start to feel really annoyed with her and find yourself
giving her the cold shoulder when you run into her at
church or the community pool. In these scenarios, you
have no good reason to be offended because you don't
know what your Facebook friends are talking about or
what your coworker was saying. If you aren't looking for
hidden meanings in people's words and actions, you'll be
far less likely to find things that hurt you.

**Show grace to those who offend you, knowing you
have also been shown grace in the past.** The reality
is that we have all said things about others that we
shouldn't have said. We have all put other people down.
It's important to remember this lest we become self-
righteous—too big for our britches, as we say in the
South. For example, it's likely you've posted something
on Facebook that has offended someone. I can practically
guarantee it. Instead of being offended by someone's
words or actions, choose to extend grace.

I can think of a time when I had to make this choice in my workplace. I was looking forward to a new hire coming on board. Unfortunately, she and I didn't click. From day one, she made comments toward me that left me feeling . . . well, offended. As a result of both her actions and my response, we frequently butted heads, causing our team to be less cohesive than it otherwise would have been. One day, I learned that this woman had just been injured at work. In that moment, I had to make a decision. Was I willing to extend grace to her despite how she had treated me? The choice was clear. So, a colleague and I scrambled to get some things taken care of for her, and we picked up the slack during her recovery. A short while later, my boss asked me why I had helped this woman, despite the way she had treated me. I replied, "Well, Doc, because love covers a multitude of sins." This answer comes from 1 Peter 4:8, which reads: "Above all, love each other deeply, because love covers over a multitude of sins." The Amplified Bible further explains that this means love forgives and disregards the *offenses* of others.

While I had every reason to be offended, the Lord impressed upon my heart that I had an opportunity here to "kill her with kindness." As a result, the relationship improved so that it was more professional, although we never became friends. And that's okay. We don't have to become good friends with everyone we know or work with. The happy ending is that I worked diligently to keep this woman's comments from getting to me. I extended grace to her, treating her how I would want to be treated. I worked hard to let go of the offenses. I worked hard to integrate the words of 1 Peter 4:8 into my life. And it worked. It can work for you too.

YOU CAN CHANGE!

Even after learning how to be more empathetic and extend grace, you may still be thinking, *I can't help my responses. God made me this way!* Let's take a look at personality characteristics and, ultimately, whether it's possible to change our responses to perceived offenses.

In a nutshell, there are two types of personality characteristics, and there is a simple difference between them. *Trait personality characteristics* are those we are born with; they are stable over time. *State personality characteristics* are temporary and can frequently change. Traits are hereditary and God-given, while personality states change depending upon many different factors. (Remember the analogy in chapter one about self-esteem being like the weather and self-worth being like the climate? In this case, state personality characteristics are like the weather and trait personality characteristics are like the climate.) A personality state may be temporary grief as the result of the death of a pet. Your sadness does not mean that you have a sad personality. Likewise, just because you have a positive temperament as a trait personality characteristic, it does not mean you are always happy.

Regardless of whether our personality characteristics are consistent day-to-day traits or temporary states, it *is* possible to work on areas of our personality that are causing us problems in our relationships. If you don't believe that's true, then you can throw out cognitive-behavioral therapy (the most researched form of therapy in existence) . . . and you can throw out the Word of God. The Bible makes it clear that we *can* change. Romans 12:2 tells us we can be transformed by the renewing of our minds. Whether you typically react to offenses in a manner consistent with your personality traits (some people are consistently calm, others are consistently hot-headed, for example) or whether you typically react to offenses based on your mood on a particular day, it is possible to change your response to offenses.

At this point, you might be thinking, *But she was rude!* Or, *but you don't know my mother-in-law—or sister, friend, or whoever.* I certainly don't know the people in your life, but I am writing to *you*. You see, you are the only person you can control. You can't change anyone else, nor can any of us. If, however, you are willing to work on developing empathy and extending grace, you can break the bad habit of being easily offended. You can learn to let go of the offense, regardless of what the other person does or doesn't do.

LET IT GO

One of my favorite Disney movies is *Frozen*. Most people have heard the song "Let It Go" more times than they can count (and perhaps more times than they cared to). While this expression was used before the movie came out, it became a cultural catchphrase after the movie's release. Really, this phrase can be a simple but effective reminder to tell yourself when you need to get over an offense. In order to get to the place where you can "let it go," ask yourself the following questions:

1. What is the offense?
2. Will it matter a year from now? Yes_____ No_____
3. Will it matter a month from now? Yes _____ No_____
4. Will it matter a week from now? Yes_____ No_____
5. Will it matter tomorrow? Yes _____ No _____
6. Will letting this offense go help or harm the relationship? Help _____ Harm _____
7. How will it harm or help?
8. Is this something I can let go? Yes _____ No _____
   (*Don't forget to pray about this decision!*)

   If you answered no, what other solutions can you use to overcome the offense?

   _____

   _____

   _____

If you answered yes to the last question, congratulations. (You can thank me later for getting "Let It Go" stuck in your head *again*.) Throughout our lives we are presented with all sorts of opportunities to take offense. For example, I've heard from many women about all the comments they received when pregnant. One told of a relative who asked to stand next to the woman in a photo so she would look thin. Another mentioned a friend who asked her if she was having twins (she wasn't!). And yet another, who was actually pregnant with twins, said she heard the comment, "Better you than me" more than once. (Her reply? "I agree!")

In these situations and many others, we can choose whether to take offense. The other person may very well have been rude or insensitive, and it may be something that needs to be addressed, but it does not help our relationships when we allow others to hurt our feelings. It also takes a toll on our emotional well-being. At some point, we have to take stock of the situation and realize that we can choose to extend grace and let go of an offense.

It's also important to be able to talk straight to those who offend us. We'll look at that in the next chapter.

WORKING ON MYSELF

Let's take some time to work on developing empathy. I'll provide the same three questions we explored in the chapter, along with space for you to write out your responses. Think of a particular person who has offended you, put yourself in that person's shoes, and answer these questions.

1. What is it like to be this person?

    _____

    _____

    _____

2. Why might this person have treated me the way he or she did?

_____

_____

_____

3. How might this person want to be treated in return?

_____

_____

_____

4. Finally, write about how you can extend grace to this person.

_____

_____

_____

Dear Lord,

I'm sorry for how I've offended others. I ask that You reveal to me if there is anyone I need to make things right with. At the same time, I ask that You help me know when and how to let go of offenses against me. Help me be more empathetic to others. And when someone else offends me, enable me to give that person grace in the way You have shown me grace. Please help me respond in a way that helps rather than harms my relationships.

Thank you, Jesus!

Amen

4

Talk Straight

A s a therapist, I've frequently heard reasons (or excuses) why a client could not (or would not) address a problem in a relationship:

"It won't make a difference."

"She won't listen to me."

"He doesn't really care what I think."

I believe the root of the issue for all of these people was fear: fear of conflict, fear of emotional turmoil, fear of losing the relationship. These fears hold many of us back from talking straight and from being honest and assertive with the people in our lives. This certainly was the case for Jane.

Jane was a highly educated, successful professional. Few knew about the challenges she had long faced with her family, particularly with her mother. The two simply did not get along. Jane was an only child and had long felt like she was her mother's caregiver instead of the other way around. She blamed her mother for a traumatic experience she had faced early in life, and consequently felt bitter and angry toward her and frequently avoided her. When they were together, Jane and her mother constantly bickered over every little thing. But, lately, things had gotten worse. Something had to give.

It was past time for Jane to address her hurt with her mother, but she couldn't bring herself to tell her mother her thoughts and feelings about the past or the current state of their relationship. Jane knew it was important, but she feared the backlash and turmoil it might cause. Most of all, she was afraid of making the situation worse. Jane realized she needed professional help, and that's why she came to see me.

Can you relate? How adept are you at talking straight with those who have hurt or offended you? When we don't talk straight, it can cause lots of problems in our relationship, so let's take a more in-depth look at this issue.

WHY IT'S IMPORTANT

When we don't talk straight about something that is bothering us, we often suffer in silence. For most of us, that can only last for so long. Like a pressure cooker without a release valve, we are likely to explode—usually in anger. And if that doesn't happen, we may just shut down and allow the relationship to phase out without even trying to see if the other person is willing to try to communicate clearly with us.

Not only that, but if we feel there is too much risk involved in being direct and honest with someone, then we have to question how *real* the relationship is. After all, if we don't talk straight with each other, that means we don't know each other's true thoughts and feelings, and we are less likely to get our needs met or to meet the needs of the other person. This was the case for Jane and her mom, and why much of my time with Jane was focused on teaching her how to communicate what she was feeling and what she needed from her mother. She needed her mother to listen to her; to acknowledge her pain; to hold her and weep with her. And in order for her mother to meet those needs, Jane needed to be able to express those needs to her.

Talking straight doesn't mean telling everyone our every thought; it means speaking up for the sake of our relationships, so that they will be stronger, healthier, and more likely to last. It means that we don't "go along to get along," but that we are willing to be vulnerable with others (to varying degrees depending on the type of relationship; for example, you're going to be more transparent with your spouse than with your boss). Talking straight not only helps to address conflict, it can help prevent it. Our bonds can be healthier and stronger—we can experience more positive feelings toward one another and less conflict—when we are willing to take the risk of talking straight.

IT'S TIME TO TALK STRAIGHT

While we cannot control how someone else reacts to us, we can work on communicating in a way that does not intentionally trigger that person's temper. It's the other side of the offense coin. On one side, we work hard not to be offended, while on the other side, we work hard not to offend. At the same time, if we talk straight we can feel better about our interactions with others, *even if the outcome is not what we desired.*

In this section, we are going to explore three paths that lead us toward talking straight to those who have hurt or angered us. We'll start with learning how to calm down. Then we'll move into learning how to communicate clearly (including a discussion on when *not* to text). Finally, we'll wrap up by seeing what the Bible has to say about taming the tongue (and not gossiping, because that does nothing but harm our relationships). Let's get started.

Calm Down

Calm down. If you're like me, just reading those words triggers defensiveness. Almost as much as "stop acting crazy." *Almost.* My friends and I were talking about this one day when one said that her husband knows never to say those words to her because they always have the exact opposite effect. (Isn't that always the case?) But here's the thing: if you are angry and upset, you are likely to say things that set off the person you are in conflict with, making it far less likely that you will be heard or understood. That's why it is never a good idea to say things in the heat of the moment.

My favorite ways to calm down include *breathing retraining* and *personal time-out*. These are simple but effective techniques to help you become less frustrated and more in control of yourself so that you can communicate as clearly and effectively as possible.

Breathing Retraining

This is an easy three-step process. Go ahead and take a few minutes to practice breathing retraining now:

1. Take a deep breath through your nose and hold your breath to the count of three.

2. Slowly let the breath out through your mouth while thinking of a calming word such as *relax*, *peace*, or *Jesus*.

3. Repeat until you feel calm.

Personal Time-Out

Anyone who has reared or worked with children is familiar with the concept of *time-out*. When a child misbehaves, a parent or other caregiver disciplines the child by relegating them to a chair or quiet spot for a specified amount of time. What I'm suggesting really is not much different. It's just the adult version. Here, you are choosing to take a time-out rather than being forced to take one. It's ideal to take a personal time-out before things get heated with someone. For example, you recognize your need to calm down before having a serious conversation with your teenager over the failing grade on his report card or before calling a meeting with the employee that you love but who has been late to work three times in the last month.

If you are already in communication with someone and realize you need to take a personal time-out, explain that you need some time to calm down before continuing. For example, you might say to your daughter: "I'm getting frustrated. Before this gets too heated, I'd like to take some time to calm down and gather my thoughts." Then, spend time doing something that reduces your stress—pray, journal, listen to music, take a walk . . . these are just a few examples. What else can you think of that might help you calm down during a personal time-out?

Calming down is essential to talking straight, but we also need to learn how to communicate clearly.

Communicate Clearly

I think back on the often-quoted cellphone carrier commercial where the guy tries to demonstrate how great the coverage is—you know the one. He carries his cellphone far and wide, high and low, often asking the person on the other end of the line, "Can you hear me now?" In order for people to truly hear us, we have to communicate effectively.

To do that, it helps to know your communication style, and whether it is the best style for talking straight. There are four different types of communication—aggressive communication, passive communication, passive-aggressive communication, and assertive communication. (Keep in mind that communication is both verbal and nonverbal.)

Aggressiveness

When you are aggressive, you are forceful in your communication. For instance:

- You raise your voice or yell at others.
- You get up close to the person, wag your finger in his or her face, or stand with your arms crossed or your hands on your hips.
- You speak harshly to someone through your tone of voice or the words you use.

When this is your style of communication, your body language and tone of voice (sometimes literally) scream that what you have to say is more important than the other person or what they have to say. Imagine for a moment that I am standing over you as you are sitting on the couch, wagging my finger in your face and yelling. If I cared about what you had to say, I sure wouldn't be showing it like this. Rather, my aggressiveness is telling you to *listen. To. Me.*

One of my former clients didn't recognize the impact her aggressiveness had on her family until she completed an activity that involved asking her husband and kids how they saw her when she was forceful—and how it made them feel. That wake-up call helped her see that by speaking loudly and harshly and using threatening body language, she was pushing her family away. Her kids were often afraid of her, and her husband often avoided her. You see, being aggressive rarely wins others to your side, unless the sheer force you are using intimidates someone into agreeing with you. Dominating others into submission does not help build healthy bonds. But it can become your go-to behavior if you're not careful. This woman was so used to being aggressive that it had become a habit for her, one that she desperately wanted to break.

Is aggressiveness your communication style some, or even

all, of the time? If so, ask yourself whether you want others to be intimidated by you. This style makes it difficult to communicate with others in a way that helps the relationship. When you are aggressive, it likely triggers defensiveness and prevents people from really hearing you.

Passiveness

When someone is being overly submissive, they are being passive. For example, a friend blames you for something that wasn't your fault, and you don't speak up for yourself. Or, a family member consistently says hurtful things to you, and even though you don't like it, you don't let him or her know how you are feeling.

When we are passive in instances where we should not be, we send the message that the other person is more important than we are, because we are putting that person's needs before our own. I've found that this can be a bit confusing for Christians, particularly women, because we have been taught to be selfless—to put others first. Yet, it is possible to put others first without becoming a doormat—someone who is walked on or taken advantage of. When we act passively, we can feel insignificant, like we just don't matter.

If you know people who are passive, you've likely been frustrated with them. You want them to express their opinions in a straightforward manner ("I would really like to meet for dinner at Luigi's. I've been wanting to eat some good Italian food.") rather than always deferring to you ("Oh, I don't know. Where do you want to go?"). While it may be fine if this kind of deference happens occasionally, if this is the pattern of communication, there is a power imbalance. Essentially, both parties are not equal, with the more assertive person dominating the passive person. The assertive person is in charge, always making decisions that should be mutually decided upon—and sometimes those decisions are not ones that the passive person would have made. (Imagine, for a moment, what that would do to your emotional health!)

So, let me ask you, are you passive? Is this your communication style? Do you have a tendency to remain silent while people blame you or yell at you, even though it upsets you? Do you avoid addressing how frustrated you are that your friend is late to pick up your kids for carpool—again? Do you dread having to deal with your sister who isn't pitching in to help your ailing parents, so you just do it yourself without saying a word or acting like there's any problem? This is being passive.

I recall early in our dating relationship going out to eat at a diner with my husband. I can't remember what he ordered, but I remember it was supposed to come with bread. When the server realized she had forgotten it, she said she would go and get it. Nick replied, "No, it's okay." The server asked again, "Are you sure?" "Really, it's fine," he told her. After she walked away, he looked at me and said, "I really wanted that bread!" He didn't want to be a bother. Can you relate? The good news is there's hope. My husband has no problem asking for the bread now!

Passive-Aggressiveness

In many ways, this is the most problematic type of communication style, and leads to the most difficulties within relationships. It can also be the most challenging to identify. A simple, but accurate, definition of passive-aggressiveness is the "indirect expression of hostility."[1] Someone who is passive aggressive sends mixed messages. On the surface, there is a level of concern or agreeableness, while other signs indicate that something is wrong.

If you start to pay attention, you will notice passive-aggressiveness all around you. For instance, a girlfriend and boyfriend get into a fight via text. After a few rounds of back and forth, the girlfriend is so frustrated that she writes, "Don't worry about it. By the way, I'll return your necklace tomorrow. Goodnight." The boyfriend is left feeling confused. *Wait. How did a minor conflict turn into her wanting to return the necklace I got her for her birthday? Is she breaking up with me?*

Here's another example. You are driving home from the store when your husband mentions that you should keep a greater distance between your car and the car ahead of you. With a small smirk, you reply, "You're welcome to do the driving for us." This is a passive-aggressive response! You don't *really* want him to drive the car; you are frustrated because you feel criticized, but you stop short of telling him that.

I'll just come out and say it: if you identified any of these first three communication styles as the one that best describes you, then you will have a difficult time talking straight. Assertiveness is the type of communication you should be striving for. It is the only style that enables us to communicate effectively.

Assertiveness

Say what you mean, and mean what you say. Be honest and direct. Let people know where you stand. This is clear communication.

Let's pause and take a look at one way to be assertive. This is called the four steps of assertiveness:

1. Describe the problem to the person. Examples:

"When you cancel our plans last minute . . ."
"When you raise your voice at me . . ."
"When you are consistently late . . ."

2. Tell the person how you choose to feel about his or her behavior. Examples:

"I feel disappointed and frustrated . . ."
"I feel unloved . . ."
"I feel disrespected . . ."

3. Tell the person how his or her behavior affects you. Examples:

". . . because I no longer have plans for the evening."
". . . and grow distant from you."
". . . and my time is wasted."

4. Suggest a new behavior that you would prefer.
   Example:

"In the future, I would prefer if we could stick to our plans unless something urgent comes up."
"In the future, I would prefer if you relayed your frustration toward me without raising your voice."
"In the future, I would appreciate your being on time or at least notifying me when you are running late."

Jane used these steps in order to be assertive in her communication with her mother. One day she excitedly told me that she had talked straight with her mom for the first time in her life. I asked her to relay what she said. It went something like this: "Mom, when I try and talk with you about the past and you tell me the past is the past and don't want to discuss it, I feel like you do not care about me or the pain I have suffered. As a result, it causes me to become frustrated with you and negatively impacts our time together. I would really like to set up a time to discuss the past in-depth. I need you to be willing to listen to what I have to say without cutting me off." While we don't always get what we want, in this instance Jane's mom did agree to her request. While their relationship didn't improve overnight—even after they discussed the past situation Jane was struggling with her mom over—they are continuing to work on their relationship. Jane feels more at peace and in less turmoil over their relationship since learning to be assertive with her mother. Talking straight contributed to her emotional well-being and it improved her relationship with her mom.

Don't Send Important Communication via Text

More and more, people are communicating with one another via text messages, and I want to point out that talking straight is difficult—if not impossible—via texting. I learned this the hard way. A loved one was making an important decision that would impact me and asked for my feedback via text. I tried to be empathetic and supportive in my reply. The next thing I know, I am receiving her decision, again via text. The decision was not what I expected. It negatively impacted me and hurt my feelings. I stewed over this for a couple of days before I decided to call her. By the time our phone call was over, we realized that she had taken my reply as encouraging her in the direction she wound up going—when that wasn't my intention at all!

The moral of this story? *Important communication should never take place via text.* Setting up a time and place to meet for dinner? Sure. Passing along an urgent prayer request to several people at once? Of course. A casual chat? No problem. But if we are trying to work through an issue, communication needs to be clear. Face to face is the best way to have serious conversations, particularly when working through conflict. If this isn't a possibility, try using Skype or FaceTime. If all else fails, an old-fashioned telephone call is your best bet.

If we want our relationships to be healthy and our bonds strong, learning to talk straight involves more than learning how to calm down and communicate clearly when we have been hurt or offended. It's also about being aware of how powerful our words are and using them to build up rather than tear down. That's where we're going next.

Tame the Tongue . . . Stop the Gossip

The tongue is a muscular, sensory organ that has 2,000–10,000 taste buds and can detect salty, sour, bitter, savory, and sweet tastes.[2] But the tongue has much more power than the ability to taste food. It has the power to give death and life (Prov. 18:21). The first twelve verses of James 3 are devoted to this small part of the body. I'll share James 3:5–10 here:

> Likewise, the tongue is a small part of the body, but it makes great boasts. Consider what a great forest is set on fire by a small spark. The tongue also is a fire, a world of evil among the parts of the body. It corrupts the whole body, sets the whole course of one's life on fire, and is itself set on fire by hell.
>
> All kinds of animals, birds, reptiles and sea creatures are being tamed and have been tamed by mankind, but no human being can tame the tongue. It is a restless evil, full of deadly poison.
>
> With the tongue we praise our Lord and Father, and with it we curse human beings, who have been made in God's likeness. Out of the same mouth come praise and cursing. My brothers and sisters, this should not be.

This passage is incredibly rich, as we learn that the tongue can be used for both praising God and causing evil. What's remarkable (and scary) to me is the statement that no human being can tame the tongue. It might be tempting to just give up, to take a defeatist attitude that if the tongue can't be tamed, why try? Well, we don't get off that easy. Instead, we have to tame our tongues. James 3:1–12 gives great insight into this. A key way to tame the tongue is by stopping the gossip, which often falls under that nasty category of passive-aggressiveness. Straight talk means speaking the truth in love. With gossip, there is no love. Yet, it's all around us.

A friend invited me to her church for a special women's event. I happened to arrive earlier than she did, so I loitered around the meeting room, waiting on her. After I decided to return to the door to see if she had arrived, I rounded a corner and came upon two church members. When they saw me, one stated, "Excuse us, we're in the middle of a gossip session."

Regardless of what those women were gossiping about, it was wrong. It seems to me that people define gossip in different ways. Some believe that something is not gossip as long as it's true. Sorry, but this is incorrect. The dictionary offers a number of definitions, but two are the most relevant to us:

1. Rumor or talk of a personal, sensational, or intimate nature.

2. A person who habitually spreads intimate or private rumors or facts.

These definitions tell us that gossip can be an *act* or a person. What strikes me is the last word: *facts*. The truth is, you can be gossiping simply by spreading facts about others that are not your business to share. If you want to reclaim relationships, gossip is not going to get you there! All too often, we go to friends to "vent" about other people: a spouse, another friend, a coworker, a boss, a neighbor, a sister/brother, a parent . . . whoever! It's one thing to go to a trusted, wise friend to pray together and ask for wise counsel. It's another thing to spread details about someone's personal business or to talk negatively about someone behind that person's back. Of course, we're all guilty of doing this from time to time, but it's important to our relationships to avoid this temptation. How can we do that? Here are three quick tips:

1. When you hear people start to gossip, don't participate. Walk away, if possible. If not, distance yourself from the conversation (turn and talk to another person nearby, read a book, pull out your phone, and so on).

2. Find a way to shut down the gossip. ("Hey, friend, I'm
   really not comfortable talking about Sally's fight with
   her boyfriend. I'll be praying for them though!")
3. Don't repeat what you heard!

Proverbs 11:13 and 20:19 both say, "Gossip betrays a confidence." (See the importance?) Yes, it does, and once trust is broken,
it is difficult (and sometimes impossible) to gain back. Proverbs
13:3 tells us that if we guard our lips, we guard our life. We *preserve*
our life. You don't do any favors for yourself and your relationships
when you gossip. Instead, if you have a problem with an individual
or a concern about that person, talk straight to him or her, and
allow that person to share his or her own business.

A CAUTIONARY TALE

Sitting in a Bible study at a friend's house one night, I was surprised
to hear someone say, "We need to pray for Brandon and Stephanie.
Can you believe they're getting divorced? Shame on him for what
he is doing to her." I was shocked by the news, and sat quietly, taken
aback that it had been shared in the manner that it was and surprised
by the person who carried on about the accusations against Brandon.
Naturally, friends were upset for this couple we knew and loved. Yet,
it felt like gossip—and if it acts like a duck and quacks like a duck . .
. you know the rest! I was disappointed by the information that had
just been shared, and also disappointed in my friends for the way
they were carrying on. Thankfully, someone in the group stopped
and said, "Y'all, can we just stop and pray for Brandon and Stephanie? Then, let's dive into our Bible study." I was happy to oblige.

Since this was the first I'd heard this news, I felt like I needed
to check it out for myself with Stephanie. So, I nervously called her
to chat. When I calmly shared what I'd heard, she thanked me for
coming to her directly. She knew about the whispered (or loudly

spoken) questions, and was weary from all the gossip. She filled me in on her family's situation, and again, thanked me for not participating in the gossip. While it was true that she and her husband were getting divorced, it was still a private matter, and she was not ready for it to be spread around our community. She was hurt by friends who chose not to tame their tongues, who chose to pass her personal news off as a prayer request (to be sure, many *were* praying). As time went on, Stephanie was able to rebuild some of her relationships, especially with those who had honestly and directly communicated with her, but the friendships that were harmed by the gossip were never repaired.

Every time I remember this cautionary tale, I'm reminded of the importance of communicating clearly, taming my tongue, and not gossiping. I'm reminded of the importance of talking straight so that my relationships will be strong. I pray it offers the same reminder to you.

WORKING ON MYSELF

1. Review the description of each of the four communication styles. Which one describes your typical communication style? Write about that below. Your style may or may not fit neatly into one of the four styles listed above.

_____

_____

_____

2. How has your conversation style impacted your relationships?

_____

_____

_____

3. Take some time to reflect on your relationships. Is there someone with whom you need to be more assertive? Take the time to work through the four steps to assertive communication, so that you can talk straight with this person and get your relationship on a more secure footing.

   Step 1: When you _____

   _____

   Step 2: I chose to feel _____

   _____

   Step 3: Because your behavior _____

   _____

   Step 4: In the future I would prefer that you _____

   _____

Dear Lord,

You know the person and situation I've been struggling with. I pray that You will be with my loved one. Show _____ Your love, and allow me to be more loving toward _____ with Your strength. Please help our relationship to improve. Show me what work I need to do on my end to help things change. Help me be assertive instead of aggressive, passive, or passive-aggressive, and to tame my tongue.

Thank You for the guidance You give me through Your Holy Word and the Holy Spirit.

In the name of Jesus,

Amen.

5

Dismiss Blame

P sychologists Henry Cloud and John Townsend say that "blamers have a character problem."[1] That is a tough pill to swallow, but it's definitely truth serum. When we blame other people for our actions, thoughts, or feelings, we aren't being honest with ourselves or others.

Humans have been blaming one another since the garden of Eden. When God confronted Eve about giving Adam some forbidden fruit that he then ate, she responded, "The serpent deceived me, and I ate" (Gen. 3:13). Now, before you think I am letting Adam off the hook, he also blamed others for his actions. Not only did he blame Eve, but he also blamed God: "The man said, 'The woman you put here with me—she gave me some fruit from the tree, and I ate it'" (Gen. 3:12).

Notice what Adam is saying here. Allow me to paraphrase. "Hey God, *You* put that woman here. And she's the one who gave me the fruit. So, really, You and Eve are to blame here, not me." Eve wasn't having that. Like Adam, she wasn't going to accept responsibility, and so she passed the buck to the serpent. She too was being dishonest. Sure, the serpent had deceived her, but she was also responsible for her actions, just like Adam was responsible for his.

As a result of their sin of disobedience, Adam and Eve suffered consequences, including a strain on their relationship as described in Genesis 3:16, "Your desire will be for your husband, and he will rule over you."

Sin has resulted in a strain on relationships since the garden. In this chapter we'll be exploring how you can break this bad habit and begin to take responsibility for your actions and the problems they may cause. We'll start with the wisdom of surrounding yourself with friends who will tell you the truth.

"FEEL GOOD" FRIENDS VS. TRUTHFUL FRIENDS

I'm on your side. But that doesn't mean I'll always agree with you. I care about you too much to pretend with you—or lie to you. So, when you tell me that the argument was your boyfriend's fault or that your friend was "definitely" in the wrong, expect me to listen intently and hold me accountable to being sensitive and compassionate, but don't look for me to automatically agree with you. Maybe I'll agree with parts of your story. I may even be able to put myself in your shoes and see things from your point of view. But, perhaps, I can also understand the other person's side. It's not hard to find someone who will agree with us all the time. I call those people "feel good" friends. And they let us out of taking responsibility.

We all love being agreed with. Being told we're right. That we look good ("No, those pants don't make your rear end look big."). The problem isn't encouragement or support from friends. The problem is when friends lie to us to make us feel good, to stay on our good side, or, worst of all, because they don't believe they can be honest with us without us getting upset or even ending our friendship. While it's easy to find someone to agree with you, it's not easy to find a truthful friend, one who challenges you to take personal responsibility for your actions instead of blaming others.

It might not seem like it, but "feel good" friendships can be harmful. Think about it. Let's say you have a problem and are seeking wisdom on how to handle the situation. You go to a friend who agrees with you about everything. She's your advocate! Your cheerleader! Your "you go, girl!" girl. But consider this: What if she's wrong? Or, maybe I should say, what if *you're* wrong? What if the problem is really of your making? What if you need to be gently and lovingly told that? And what if that feel-good friend isn't truthful about it?

Your feel-good friend likely means well. In fact, she may see things your way and may not be withholding her true opinion. But what we all need are friends who are willing and able to look at all sides of a situation prayerfully and thoughtfully instead of jumping to our defense. The latter can cause us more difficulty in the long run. When we're not challenged to take responsibility, most of the time we don't—and that leads to us playing the blame game, which is precisely what we want to avoid.

START TAKING RESPONSIBILITY

Imagine you can't find your keys. You just *know* your husband moved them because you are positive you left them on the kitchen counter, and since he cleaned up the kitchen, he must have put them somewhere. He insists he didn't touch your keys, but you remain irritated with him because you are sure he did something with them. Thirty minutes later, you put on your coat to go outside for a walk—and discover your keys in the pocket.

Now imagine it's he who misplaced his keys and blamed you instead of the other way around. We only need to consider a time when we've been blamed for someone else's actions to know that this is no fun.

When I was a little girl, my sister and I were in the bedroom we shared. She had fallen asleep by the time our parents came in to check on us. One of them (I won't say which parent) opened the door and noticed the stuffing from my sister's doll all over the floor. Since my older (and less rambunctious) sister was asleep, guess who got the blame for pulling the innards out of that doll? You guessed it—me. I insisted I had not done the dirty deed, and thankfully when she woke up, my sister told the truth and owned up to the fact that she had pulled out the doll's insides (thanks, sis!).

It would have been easier for my sister if she had passed the buck. If she hadn't been honest, I would have been punished—and been angry with both my sister and Dad (oops). This time, my sister accepted responsibility. Still, during my growing up years, I know my parents heard "She started it," "Blame her," and "It's her fault" more times than they can count (I am one of five children). We're all adults now and know the right thing to do. The same is true for you.

I wonder how many relationships would improve if we were willing to look at our part in the problems we may be having in our relationships. If we started saying things like:

"It's my fault."

"I was wrong."

"I'm to blame."

Would marriages strengthen if, instead of blaming each other, we examined the role we may have played in the conflict? If we accepted responsibility first, instead of giving our spouse the cold shoulder or waiting for him to come to us?

Would parents and teenagers get along better if both admitted they needed to work harder at understanding one another instead of constantly claiming the other one "just doesn't understand"?

Would coworkers have less stressful relationships if they stopped pointing the finger at the other when something goes wrong at the office?

Remember the example about the wife who blamed her

husband for the keys she lost in her own pocket? My husband and I
used to be that couple. Now, instead of blaming each other for misplaced items and the like, we have learned to ask questions such as,
"Have you seen my keys?" and accepting the answer when it's "no"
rather than accusing the other of moving them. Or when we don't
know who, for example, left the refrigerator door open, Nick will
often accept responsibility: "I think I left the fridge open. I need
to remember to double check the door." By using "I" statements
like these, instead of casting blame, he is reminding both of us to
be mindful of what we are doing. Not only does this prevent argu-
ments and hurt feelings, it also motivates us to be more careful in
the future. (Note: Nick does not take responsibility for things that
are clearly not his fault, but more often than not we don't know
who had the remote last or who left the top off the toothpaste.)

I have a hunch things would be better in our relationships if we
spent more time reflecting on our own junk and owning it rather
than looking for someone else to blame. The question is: How? How
do we stop blaming others and start taking responsibility? I want
to provide three ideas for you. We'll unpack them here, and you'll
have space to practice them for yourself at the end of the chapter.

Accept and Own Your Responsibility

Sometimes, one person is clearly to blame. All the responsibility should fall on his or her shoulders—for example, when a colleague lies, a teenager breaks curfew, or a spouse has an affair. In
these cases, the person who is clearly in the wrong needs to own
his or her actions.

But more often than not, there is plenty of blame to go around.
When you are in conflict with someone, ask yourself, "What is
my level of responsibility here? Am I am partly or solely responsible? What have I done to contribute to this conflict? How am I
responsible?"

For example, let's say you are searching for a new car. You ask your dad to help you find the right car within your budget, and he agrees to do so. He tells you which kinds of cars he thinks you should consider, and which to avoid. A few days later you learn that a friend of a friend has a car for sale that sounds like a good buy. When you ask your dad to come with you to check out the car, he refuses because the make of the car is one he warned you about. So you go on your own to look at the car and fall in love with it instantly. Right on the spot you decide not to follow your dad's advice, and you purchase the car without getting it checked out by a mechanic.

When you tell your dad you bought the car, he says he is not going to help you if it breaks down. Your retort is "Fine, I'll handle it myself." Life goes on . . . until the car breaks down in the middle of a busy road two weeks after your purchase, and you call your dad for help. Of course, he comes to help you out, but he is upset with you for not taking his advice. You're also upset with him because you figure if he had come with you, he might have been able to tell there was something wrong with the car before you made the purchase. You each blame the other for the situation. Let's take a look at your possible level of responsibility:

> *On a scale of 0–100, what is my level of responsibility? Well, I am certainly not 0 percent responsible. I also don't feel 100 percent responsible because my dad said he would help me through the car-buying process to the end—and he didn't. Still, I am an adult now, and I went against his advice. That makes me mostly responsible. I ignored his advice and failed to get the car properly checked out before purchasing it. It's not his fault that I bought a lemon, and he is not to blame. I am responsible for getting angry with him when he was trying to help me.*

Once you've identified your level of responsibility, it's time to own it. For example, in the car mishap with your dad, you might respond, "I don't have a right to get upset with you since I did not listen to your advice about the car. Thank you for offering to help me and for coming to my aid when it broke down. In the future, I won't ask for your help unless I'm going to follow your advice. I'll work harder not to blame you for my mistakes."

Pray for Discernment and Guidance

Ask God to give you the wisdom to know how you can right your wrongs. Do you need to admit your wrongdoing to someone? Ask for forgiveness? Make amends some other way?

Keep in mind that if you have sinned, repentance will be an important part of your prayer. Apologies and forgiveness are a critical part of resetting relationships that have been broken. Confession, repentance, and forgiveness are integral to staying in right fellowship with God and having a healthy relationship with others. (We'll talk more about these concepts in a later chapter.)

Own Your Feelings

Taking responsibility includes owning our own feelings—acknowledging that no one can "make" us feel a particular way.

When I used to facilitate anger management groups, I often heard the expression, "He made me mad," or "It's her fault I got angry." My question in response is this: "Did someone hold you down, pin you against the floor, and tell you that you could not get up until you got mad?" Now, I know that being pinned down against my will would make me mad, but you get the point. No one *makes* us get mad. No one makes us have any emotion. Others can trigger our emotions, but they cannot force us to feel anger or depression or impatience. The same is true for our thoughts.

Did you know that before every feeling is a thought? Often,

this process happens so quickly that we are not aware of a particular thought. The likely scenario is that something happens (point "a") and then you have an emotion (point "b"), but between point "a" and point "b" is a thought. There are many times in life when we experience negative events that appropriately lead to negative thoughts that lead to negative feelings. For instance, when a loved one dies, we think, *I won't see her again until I get to heaven,* and we feel sad. That is natural and healthy. Yet, there are other times when our negative thoughts do not align with the event. In therapeutic circles, this kind of negative thinking is sometimes called "stinking thinking." And what do you think stinkin' thinkin' leads to? Yep, negative feelings. We feel crummy even when our feelings are not in line with what happened. So we turn it around; we blame someone else for how we feel. That blame serves as nothing but a wedge between us and a loved one.

Let me give you a couple of examples of how stinkin' thinkin' can lead to blaming others for how we feel, and then show you how the people in these examples could have taken ownership of their feelings:

Two out of three roommates aren't getting along. They get into another big fight, and the third is torn between her two friends and finds herself getting upset with both of them. She thinks, *This is exactly like what my parents did to me. They put me in the middle of their fights all the time.* She feels anxious, just like she did as a child. Her anger at her friends indicates that she is blaming them for making her feel upset and uncomfortable.

If she were to own her feelings, her response would be quite different. She might think: *Their fight is not my problem. I do not have to choose between them. I can still communicate with both of them and leave their reconciliation up to them. I am choosing not to worry about this.* As a result, she may still feel anxious, but she wouldn't blame her friends for her anxiety.

The coleaders of the drama team at the community theater are having creative differences. They cowrote a play, but couldn't agree on a title. After thinking about it, one emails the other and expresses her strong feelings about going with the title she liked. The email infuriates the coleader. "If you feel so strongly about this, we should be talking face to face instead of sending emails. I'll talk with you at the next meeting." She stews over the situation the entire week. *She thinks she's in charge. Well, she's not. I'm going to make sure she knows that!* This line of thinking only serves to fuel the flame of her anger.

Instead, she could have thought, *I do not like her insistence that we go with the title she likes, but I need to give her a chance to list her reasons. I am going to choose not to be upset about this. This is not the end of the world. Nothing tragic has happened. We can talk about it at our next meeting.*

Notice how in the alternate responses the situation didn't change—only the thoughts and feelings changed. That is what we have control over. Isn't it freeing to know we do have control? That we can take responsibility for these things instead of blaming others?

In this next section we'll look at what we can do when we are the ones on the receiving end of blame.

CONFRONTING BLAMERS

Henry Cloud and John Townsend remind us that if someone is "trying to blame you for something they should take responsibility for, confront them."[2] They go on to provide an example of a brother who asks his sister for money for his business. When she doesn't lend it to him (as a result of lending him money in the past that was never returned), he blames her for his business going downhill. The sister confronts him and basically tells him, "Your career is your responsibility, not mine. Please do not blame me."[3]

Taking responsibility for your actions does not mean allowing other people to blame you unjustly. The practice activity at the end of this chapter will help you think through who you might need to confront and what you might say to the blamer in your life. Let me give you one more example to get you thinking in that direction.

Imagine your husband frequently leaves the house at the last minute, racing out the door to get to work on time. He sets his alarm but always turns it off. He doesn't ask you to make sure he's up, but you often do because you want him to get to work on time; you don't want him to lose his job. His portion of the household income makes a big difference in the family budget.

One beautiful spring morning, you wake up early and go for a run. You lose track of time as you stop along the jogging trail, taking photos of the beautiful blooming flowers. When you arrive home, sweaty and ready to jump in the shower, you realize your husband is still sleeping. Glancing at the clock, you see he should have left for work an hour ago. You wake him up: "Honey, get up! Now! You are an hour late to work!" He jumps out of bed, throws on his clothes, and while he's racing out the door, he yells, "Thanks a lot for not waking me up!"

You don't hear from him all day, and you're worried about how his boss reacted to your husband's tardiness. At the same time, you're hot under the collar over his comment to you. *How can he blame me? He's a grown man. It's his responsibility to get himself up for work. Not mine. He's not one of the kids, but he sure is acting like it.* The day drags on, and your husband finally comes storming in the door. Still angry, he says "Thanks to you, I got in big trouble at work today."

How might you react to this uncalled-for blaming? Here's an

example of an emotionally healthy response: "I'm sorry you were late to work today. I know you are used to me waking you up when you sleep past your alarm; however, waking you up is not my responsibility. It is your fault you woke up late, it is your fault you got to work late, and it is your fault you got in trouble with your boss. In the future, I will not be waking you up." This offers your husband a chance to realize the fault lies with him.

Of course, there is no guarantee that your confronting him will diminish his anger at you. Again, if we want to stay emotionally healthy in the midst of messy relationships, we will recognize and accept that we have no control over another person's reactions— only our own. (*A word of caution*: I am not encouraging people in abusive relationships to confront an abuser; at least, not without professional assistance. If you are in an abusive situation, please seek help immediately.)

Who Hit Whom?

If you've had kids, been around kids, or been a kid yourself, you know how children blame one another. They don't want to accept responsibility for their own actions. They want to avoid punishment. They may even want to avoid disappointing the adult who is correcting them. I have two nephews. One time when they were riding in my back seat, I heard a noise that was unmistakably one hitting the other. I immediately asked who hit whom. They both blamed the other. To this day, I don't know which child hit the other one.

Sadly, we adults are often no better than the children we once were. We blame other people. We don't want to accept responsibility. We don't want to receive our punishment. We don't want to disappoint others. But blaming others keeps us emotionally stunted and only serves to hinder our relationships. It causes us to become angry, bitter, and distant from one another. If you want relationships that are healthy and satisfying, you'll commit to the work of learning to accept responsibility for your actions, thoughts, and feelings, and to stop playing the blame game.

WORKING ON MYSELF

1. What is my level of responsibility? Using a current or past situation, write about your level of responsibility below. On a scale of 0–100, where 0 is no responsibility and 100 is sole responsibility, what is your level of responsibility? How are you responsible?

   _____

   _____

   _____

2. What can I do to stop blaming someone and start taking responsibility? Using the same example from the first question, write out what you plan to do to stop blaming someone else and start taking responsibility.

   _____

   _____

   _____

3. Pray for discernment and pray for guidance. Below, write out your prayer.

   _____

   _____

   _____

4. If someone is blaming you for something that he or she should be taking responsibility for, consider confronting this person about this. What might you say?

_____

_____

_____

Dear Lord,

Not only do I blame others, but I have faced the blame of others. Please convict me when I am playing the blame game and refusing to take responsibility for my actions. Give me the strength to do what is right. I pray, too, that those I am in relationship with will be able to see the way they hurt others with their blame games. If they have been hurt as a result of blame, I ask that they find freedom from that pain.

In the name of Jesus,

Amen.

6

Eradicate Envy

King Solomon didn't play around. When his mother, Bathsheba, asked him to allow his half-brother, Adonijah to marry Abishag, one of Solomon's attendants, Solomon had Adonijah killed. Here's the story (see 1 Kings 1–2).

When King David was old and close to death, his son Adonijah hatched a plot so that he would be crowned king. He invited all his brothers—except for Solomon—and the commanders of his father's army to a banquet, where the guests all shouted, "Long live King Adonijah!" When Solomon, the son destined to be king, found out, he took back the crown and spared Adonijah's life. But Adonijah wasn't done trying to get what he wanted. His envy and greed led him down another path of deceit. This time, he tried to use Solomon's mother by asking her to make the above request to the king for him. For whatever reason, Bathsheba agreed (I'm thinking she didn't really know the implications of the request). But, why in the world did Solomon give orders for Adonijah to be killed, all because he wanted to marry Abishag?

I believe that Solomon recognized Adonijah's motives. The truth was, Adonijah didn't really want to marry Abishag. What he wanted was a foothold into the kingdom through this woman who was a part of King David's harem. If Adonijah married her, he could

wind up inheriting the kingdom, as only a king could take posses-
sion of a deceased king's servants. Solomon knew the threat that
his half-brother posed, so he had him killed.

Adonijah's envy and greed led him to try and force things to
go the way he wanted them to go. He wanted the life that God had
given Solomon, and he hatched a couple of failed plots to secure
that life. But his plans didn't work, which should be a warning to us.

We too want what others have. We too want to do what others
do for a living. We want their relationships, their looks, their popu-
larity, their status—we want to live the lives God has planned for
other people. But when we are jealous of someone, it erodes our
emotional well-being and makes it impossible to have a healthy or
satisfying relationship with that person. This was true for Adonijah. His envy of his brother Solomon destroyed the trust between
him and his brother and between him and his father, King David.
Ultimately, jealousy led Adinojah to his own demise.

I'm not usually a fan of the "What If?" game, but sometimes
it just fits, like right now. *What if* we stopped trying to be other
people? *What if* we stopped wanting what they have? *What if* we
stopped trying to get around God's plan only to force our own?
What if we opened ourselves to God's will and left the outcomes of
our lives up to Him?

Letting go of our jealousy can open up a world of freedom that
we didn't even know was possible. Just think of what might have
happened if Cain had not allowed his jealousy to lead him down the
path of killing his brother Abel.[1] Even if our jealousy doesn't ever
come close to tempting us to consider murder, it can still cause a
huge mess in our relationships. The story of the first brothers and
the story of Adonijah should give us pause. We must eradiate our
envy, and the time is now.

But before we look at how to tackle the Shakespearean-named,
green-eyed monster, let's look briefly at what it is, the types of
harm it can cause to relationships, and how social media can stoke

the fire of jealousy. (In a later chapter, I'll write more about the problems that envy causes when it leads to wanting to get even with someone.)

JEALOUSY, SIBLING RIVALRY, AND ESTRANGEMENT

Simply put, "jealousy can happen when you are afraid someone will take something from you that you want" or "when you want something another person has."[2] While we all feel jealous from time to time, habitual envy can lead us to wonder why God will "leave me empty and bless others."[3] I use the terms *jealousy* and *envy* interchangeably in this chapter, but it's common to view these as separate experiences that may happen simultaneously. Jealousy is defined as "wanting to keep what we angrily fear we might lose" and envy is defined as "wanting to gain what we do not have."[4] Jealousy and envy are twin sisters that wreak havoc in relationships. Just ask Cindy.

Cindy had been coming to see me for a while when she began opening up about her older sister, Carol, and their relationship. Growing up, the two were quite competitive with each other and both dreamed of becoming professional singers. While that didn't happen, Carol did open up a voice studio, and Cindy's teenage daughter took private lessons from her. Although Cindy had always been a bit jealous that Carol had done more with music than she had, she knew her sister was talented and trusted her to train her daughter well. Not only did Cindy's daughter see her aunt for an hour each week for her voice lessons, she also began spending a significant amount of time with her aunt outside of those lessons. Cindy became increasingly jealous of the relationship her daughter and her sister were forming. She wound up ruminating over the thought that not only did her sister have *her* dream job, she now had her daughter too.

One day, when Cindy was picking up her daughter at the

studio, she raised her voice to Carol: "I told you I didn't want her singing this kind of music." Carol retorted, "This is *my* studio, and I make the decisions around here!" Tensions mounted as Cindy replied, "Well, then, we won't be coming to *your* studio. And by the way, she is *my* daughter. Stop spending so much time with her!" With that, she grabbed her daughter by the arm and pulled her toward the door. Stunned, Carol stood there with tears streaming down her face.

Cindy decided her daughter could no longer take voice lessons from Carol—and she limited the amount of time they spent together. Her jealousy of her sister caused a rift between them that soon felt uncrossable. Carol determined that if Cindy was going to limit her access to her niece, then fine. She wouldn't see her niece at all. Not only did envy hurt these two sisters, it devastated Cindy's daughter, who missed spending time with her beloved aunt. Sadly, Carol and Cindy and their families were alienated for many years.

When Carol later developed a life-threatening illness, it was the wake-up call that Cindy needed to try and reconcile and rebuild with her sister. Thankfully, they were able to redeem their relationship before Carol's death, and aunt and niece also made up along with the other members of the two families. Nevertheless, the members of two families were estranged for years due to the envy that took root and bred discord among them.

Jealousy puts a wedge in other types of relationships as well—for instance, when an employee gets jealous that a coworker got the promotion the employee believed he or she deserved, causing the employee to feel angry and tense around his or her coworker, or when a college student feels so jealous that her friend has a new boyfriend that she stops wanting to be around her friend.

Stoking the fires of jealousy in today's society are online social media platforms. Have you noticed the impact of social media on relationships?

FACEBOOK AND
THE DEATH OF FRIENDSHIP

While I have never wanted to *be* anyone other than myself, I do sometimes find myself wishing I had something that someone else has. I want the platform of the *New York Times* bestselling author and sold-out crowd speaker. I want to be in better shape, like the woman at the gym I see every time I am there. (Note to self: perhaps that's why she is in such great shape . . . she works out a lot!) I wish I got the promotion that my colleague got even if there are clear reasons why God didn't have that for me. Her baby? Want it. His car? Want that too. As I write, I'm looking out my window at the large southern front porch across the street and wishing my smaller porch had the same width.

I think the place I tend to feel jealousy the most is Facebook. Despite knowing that what we see on Facebook is not always (okay, rarely) *real life*, it's tempting to covet what we see in perfectly posed pictures. I would bet that most of us want something that someone else has. You know what else I would bet on (if I were a betting woman)? I would bet that *you* have something someone else wants. Perhaps it's a physical feature (flat tummy?), your job (set your own hours?), or a personality trait (never meet a stranger?). The reality is that we all become envious, and most of us have something others envy. It's a vicious cycle. And while Facebook can be a great resource for reconnecting with old friends, sharing good news and prayer requests, and watching cute videos of kids and kittens, it does have a way of triggering envy that leads to detrimental effects. Let me give you an example.

Laurie was sick and tired of seeing all of her friend's good news on Facebook. Her friend's posts just made her more aware of the things she didn't have but wanted: *she* hadn't gotten the college degree; *she* hadn't gotten married; *she* didn't have a house, two kids, and a dog. Laurie tried to put on a show of being happy for her friend, but inside she wasn't. It was hard enough going to her friend's graduation party, wedding, and baby shower, but she was forced to relive everything through the photo albums, videos, and constant "congrats" on her friend's Facebook wall.

One Friday night as Laurie sat at home watching *The Golden Girls* reruns, eating ice cream, and scrolling through Facebook, she saw an "adorable" picture of her friend with her husband on a romantic night out. Throwing the spoon into the tub of ice cream that sat in her lap, Laurie decided she'd had enough. She was done with seeing all the good news on Facebook. It's not that she was terribly unhappy with her own life, but she was so envious of her friend that she couldn't see straight. She decided right then and there to "unfriend" her former BFF—and if that meant her friend would unfriend her in real life, so be it.

Not surprisingly, that's what happened. Laurie's friend reached out to her a couple of times, asking why she had unfriended her, but Laurie was too embarrassed to admit the truth. Now, when she occasionally runs into this former friend, she becomes anxious because she has a tough time admitting why she ended the friendship abruptly without so much as a word. She knew she had failed at following the Golden Rule and longed to do things differently next time. That's why she came to see me. She really wanted to get a handle on her jealousy before it ruined any more relationships.

Clearly, it's not the social media platform's fault that Laurie was jealous. And maybe Laurie's friend came across as bragging, which might get under anyone's skin. The point is that instead of admitting that she struggled with being jealous of her friend—and then doing something about it, Laurie simply ended the friendship.

Do either Carol's or Laurie's story hit close to home? When you hear about a friend's success or see his or her posts on social media, do you feel a bit envious, wanting what your friend has and feeling dissatisfied with your lot in life? If so, this next section is for you, as it explores some ways to eradicate envy from your life.

WAYS TO ERADICATE ENVY

In my experience, three of the most effective ways to eradicate envy are to:

1. Count your blessings—and others' blessings too.

2. Change your thinking

3. Accept what you can't change

Let's take a look at each of these.

Count Your Blessings—and Others' Blessings Too

One of my favorite movies is *White Christmas,* a 1950s film about two army buddies and two sisters who become entertainers. One night one of the women is having trouble sleeping. She gets up to get a glass of milk and runs into one of the men. He tells her, then sings to her, that counting her blessings (instead of sheep) will help to cure her temporary insomnia.

This advice may be put to even better use as a cure for envy. When we are thankful for our blessings, we are less likely to be jealous. For one thing, jealousy and gratitude are incompatible; as opposites, they can't coexist. Gratitude involves acknowledging the goodness in our lives.[5] Dr. Robert Emmons has conducted research that shows that grateful thoughts lead to happier feelings—by up to 25 percent![6]

Are you ready to feel less jealous and feel more grateful? If so, take some time to count your blessings. Consider your shelter (regardless of the size of your home), your clothing (regardless of the brands), and your transportation (regardless of the mode). Consider your health and healthcare. Consider your achievements (and don't let the world define them for you . . . what have you accomplished that God called you to?). Consider your education (no one can take it away . . . and this doesn't only refer to degrees) and employment (or consider your retirement or your opportunity to stay home with children full time). Consider your freedom and safety. Consider your community. Consider your family and friends. Consider your church. Most of all, consider your faith!

But don't stop there. Consider what you see in the lives of others that you can celebrate along with them. Theodore Roosevelt was right when he reportedly said, "comparison is the thief of joy." When we compare ourselves with others, it robs us of joy. We start to compete with them. This competition drives us to want to be "better than"—and to become envious when this isn't achieved. But if we can learn to truly be happy for the good things in other people's lives, we'll be far less likely to envy them for those good things.

If you struggle with jealousy, it may sound like a big leap to practicing gratitude. However, I think you'll find that once you begin to count your own blessings, you will find that it is easier to be happy on the behalf of others. Sincerely happy. Romans 12:15 tells us to "rejoice with those who rejoice." Paul knew what he was talking about. It really is important to be grateful not only for your own blessings, but for the blessings of others. When we can get to this point—even if it feels like a monumental task—we can get closer to our goal of ending envy. People who are grateful "have better relationships, are more likely to protect and preserve these relationships, are more securely attached, and are less lonely."[7] Now *these* are things to be thankful for!

Of course, the most important blessing we have to be grateful for is the gift of salvation. "In Paul's writings, there is a strong link between the awareness of grace and the resulting experience of gratitude."[8] When we focus on this amazing, free gift of forgiveness of sins and promise of eternal life, we are filled with gratitude.

Now let's talk about the second way to eradicate envy: changing your thinking.

Change Your Thinking

You might remember from chapter 1 the importance of using self-talk to combat insecurity. The idea is to replace destructive and hurtful thoughts with thoughts that are true and life-giving. Self-talk can also be a powerful therapeutic tool for helping us eradicate jealousy. We can use it to remind ourselves about God's plan for each of us rather than focusing on what He has for someone else.

Oftentimes, we believe that an event triggers a feeling, but the reality is that what we *think* about the event leads to the feeling. For example, if another couple in our circle of friends had a baby while my husband and I continued to wait years to adopt, I might have felt jealous of them. But, there is a missing component in that sentence. Something happens between the event of a couple having a baby and my feeling of envy—my thoughts. In this case, I might think, *Why does this couple who have barely been married a minute get to have children while my husband of fourteen years and I continue to wait?* If I change my thoughts, I can change my feeling. A replacement thought might be, *I am thankful that this couple does not have to experience what we have been through. I am thankful they gave birth to a healthy baby. I am thankful they are a godly couple who will raise their child in a Christian home. Plus, I bet I'll get some baby snuggles!* When I change my thinking, my jealousy eases and I can celebrate with these new parents.

When we replace a jealous, harmful thought with a realistic, helpful thought, we feel better and our relationships are less likely to suffer. Here are additional examples of how to change your thinking.

- When you are tempted to be jealous of the new gal your best friend is hanging out with, replace that thought with something like, *I am so glad _____ has another good friend. I am not always available, and I want her to have others she can depend on.*

- When you are envious that your sibling seemingly got more attention from your parents during the last holiday, replace those thoughts with something such as, *I am grateful that I still have my parents to spend time with and that I enjoy spending time together so much that it's never enough.*

- When you find the green-eyed monster rearing her ugly head while attending yet another bridal shower (while you're single and desiring marriage), think something along the lines of, *Being jealous of my friends getting what I want does not change my circumstances, and it causes me to miss out on the joy I could be experiencing by celebrating with them.*

Accept What You Can't Change

When sin gets in the way, people suffer—including us. And you know what? Envy is sin. James 3:14–15 tells us that jealousy is not wise and causes disorder. In fact, love does not envy, according to 1 Corinthians 13:4. Decide what is more important to you. Your envy/jealousy or your relationship with the person you feel jealous of? Romans 8:28 reminds us that God works all things together for good for those who love Him. If I love what others have more than I love God, I am going to miss out on the good God has prepared for me.

Sometimes, the way to eradicate these negative feelings is to accept what we can't change. *Let me clarify that I am not saying you should accept an aspect of a relationship that is harmful to you or goes against Scripture.* Adultery, abuse, addiction: these things are never acceptable. Instead, I'm reflecting on the first line in the serenity prayer: "God, grant me the serenity to accept the things I cannot change." While we are doing a lot of work to change what we can (the second line of the prayer), we can't forget that we can't change things that have already happened. What is the use of feeling jealous toward a friend whose husband is considerate and romantic—unlike yours? Or envious of a sibling who graduated with a degree in engineering and was offered his or her dream job? Or jealous of a friend who inherited a huge sum of money when her grandparents died?

If worry cannot add a single hour to our lives (Matt. 6:27), then surely envy doesn't add to our happiness or nurture strong relationships. The third line of the serenity prayer asks God to grant us the wisdom to know the difference between what we can change (such as our thinking) and what we can't always change (our circumstances). We can reduce our jealousy by accepting what we can't change.

A HOPEFUL STORY

The good news is that although jealousy causes strife in a relationship, it doesn't mean the relationship can't be reset. Take Jacob and Esau. We learn early on in their story that there was conflict between these twins from the time they were in the womb. Not only that, one parent favored one son while the other parent favored the other son (at least both parents didn't favor the same child!). This furthered the envy.

Jacob took advantage of Esau during a time of weakness, and Esau ended up giving his birthright as the firstborn to his younger brother. Later on, their mother, Rebekah, helped Jacob trick their father, Isaac, into giving Jacob the blessing that rightfully belonged to Esau. Naturally, this caused some strife between the twins, and Esau held a grudge against Jacob (Gen. 27:41). Jacob ended up fleeing for his life and lived for years in another country. Fast forward several chapters and years. In Genesis 32, Jacob is preparing to face his bitter brother after years of estrangement. Jacob was prepared for the worst, but Esau was gracious—running toward his long-lost brother, embracing him, and kissing him. Despite a past of jealousy, these brothers redeemed their relationship.

If jealousy had gotten her way, Jacob and Esau would have been permanently separated. Yet, forgiveness and grace won out. Jacob and Esau were able to set aside their envy and reunite as brothers. Jealousy and envy don't have to have the last say. We can choose to count our own blessings, count the blessings of others, and accept what we can't change. These *decisions* can help us kick the green-eyed monster to the curb.

WORKING ON MYSELF

This is going to be simple, but hard. Honesty often is. In the space below (and using extra paper if needed), tell God what's on your heart and mind. Yes, He already knows these things, but it will do your own soul good to lament and repent.

> **Lament.** This is a cry of grief. Spend some time writing about who and what you are jealous or envious of. Follow this up with your why—why do you believe you are burdened with these emotions? Be as truthful as possible.

_____

_____

_____

> **Repent.** In the Hebrew language, this word can mean "to turn" or "to regret"[9] while in the Greek language it means "to change your mind."[10] I once heard it said in a sermon that repentance is the process of dethroning sin, and enthroning God. Do you need to turn away from jealousy and envy? To admit that you've been wrong, and change your mind about your negative thoughts and feelings? Take some time to write out a prayer of repentance below.

_____

_____

_____

Comment. Here is your chance to practice changing an unhelpful, jealous thought into a helpful, positive thought that may reduce your envy and strengthen your relationship.

Jealous Thought _____

Replacement Thought _____

Jealous Thought _____

Replacement Thought _____

Jealous Thought _____

Replacement Thought _____

Dear Heavenly Father,

I know I am not alone in my struggle with jealousy and envy. This is a battle many women face, and I want to pray for those who are suffering along with me. We may keep this sin secret, not wanting to admit our jealousy, but it's real and it's eating us alive. Lord, please be with my sisters in Christ and help them to overcome these negative thoughts and feelings. I'm trusting You to do this work in their lives and in mine.

It's in the name of Jesus I pray,

Amen.

7

Forget Fear

The woman gently rocked back and forth in the chair, her arms crossed as if to cuddle herself. With her head tucked down, she didn't seem to mind the tears rolling down her cheeks and on to her denim skirt.

"I still can't believe he's gone," Avery whispered.

Avery had lost her father to cancer a few months before and had been grieving deeply ever since. But grief wasn't the only issue she was wrestling with. She and her husband had been fighting nonstop over the past several weeks. Avery explained that for a short while after her father's death her husband had been very loving and supportive, and they seemed to grow closer. But, lately, Avery found herself becoming increasingly frustrated with him.

"He said I don't think he does anything right. That I'm pushing him away. I guess he's right."

Avery recounted their most recent argument, the one she started over him leaving his shoes in the middle of the living room floor. Her husband wanted a break from the fighting; he said he was going out for a walk and some fresh air and would be back shortly. But that didn't set well with her.

"Go ahead!" she'd yelled at him. "Leave me—just like my father did."

With that, Avery once again broke down in sobs, as she felt the waves of sorrow and fear wash over her all over again.

FEAR IN RELATIONSHIPS

Fear was overwhelming Avery and crippling her ability to be connected and close to her husband. At the heart of her pushing him away was the fear that not only had she lost her father, she would lose her husband too.

Many women, like Avery, struggle with the fear of abandonment. Many women also struggle with the fear of inadequacy and the fear of rejection. Sometimes these three build on one another, with the fear of not being enough leading to the fear that a loved one will push you away, ultimately ending in a full-blown panic that the person is going to leave you altogether. Other times, circumstances like Avery's lead us directly to fear the worst.

We'll look at these three common fears, how they impact us and our relationships, and what we can do to face and ultimately forget fear.

The Fear of Inadequacy

I'm not attractive enough for him.
She likes my brother better.
I'll never be smart enough to compete with that colleague.

Thoughts like these stem from the fear that we are inadequate. We feel less than, not good enough. I recall a time when I felt exactly that way.

I sat in the bathroom crying, convinced my husband didn't love me. Nick and I hadn't even been arguing, but something triggered the thought in my mind that I wasn't *enough* for him (infertility will do that to you), and late into the night I allowed it to spin and spin until it became like a tornado, ready to destroy everything in its path. After finally calming down, I crawled into bed as quietly as possible so as not to wake Nick and reveal to him my swollen eyelids, a result of my many tears. The next day, still bothered by this nagging thought, I just had to know.

"I want to ask you a question, and I want an honest answer. Do you really love me?"

My sweet husband's eyes flew open in surprise. "Of course I do, sweetheart!" he exclaimed. "What in the world makes you ask that question?"

I was ashamed to admit it, but I had let fear of inadequacy get the better of me.

When we think we are not enough for another person, when we feel we are lacking something the other person needs or wants, we often try to prove ourselves—to prove we're worthy of being that person's spouse or friend. Ironically, even constant reassurance from the other party rarely satisfies the deep-seated fear that you will never measure up. It can be exhausting and frustrating for the other person to repeat what he or she has said to you a million times, like a song on repeat. Not to mention the pressure it places on the people in your life to constantly make sure you're okay. Don't get me wrong: relationships should be cultivated so that we see and hear one another. We should feel free to express our fears. But this doesn't mean that the other person is responsible for how we think or feel.

The only person responsible for your thoughts and feelings is you—and recognizing this is the first step in fighting this fear. Here's the thing: while others can trigger your defenses—like your self-defeating thoughts and upsetting feelings—no one else chooses what you think or how you feel. That's on you. And since you can't control anyone else, it makes sense that the way to reduce your fear if to learn to control your thoughts. Yes, we're back to self-talk. Remind yourself of what is true. Ask yourself:

What is the evidence?

Imagine you are in a courtroom. The judge is there in her black robe, gavel in hand. The lawyers are sitting in their designated chairs on either side of the courtroom. The jury of your peers sits in the jury box, staring at you as they wait for an answer. You, my friend, are in the stand. You've taken your oath. You've got to answer the questions honestly.

What is the evidence that your boss doesn't like you and won't ever give you a promotion?

What is the evidence that your friend will stop talking to you if you tell her the truth about your past?

What is the evidence that God doesn't love you, won't forgive you, or is disappointed in you?

The question I had to answer? What is the evidence that your husband doesn't love you? Truth be told, I didn't have any evidence. Zip. Zero. Blessed, I know.

Imagine me leaning in toward you here. I've got a hard, but important truth to tell you. Are you ready? Okay. Most of the time, when we analyze the evidence, we find that our fear is unjustified. But what if, when you analyze the evidence, you find proof that you were right? Maybe you can point to clear evidence that your mom likes your brother better than she likes you. Maybe the guy you longed to date and put yourself out for told you that you aren't his type. Even so, it does not mean you are inadequate. And it doesn't mean you have to allow your fear of inadequacy to spill over into other relationships.

As we move through the rest of this chapter, we'll talk about fears of rejection and abandonment. Oftentimes, these fears come from past experiences. When that's the case, we must hold on to the truth that not only is there healing from brokenness, but also hope for improved relationships going forward.

The Fear of Rejection

My client Bobbie had been rejected by her husband. She had been rejected by her daughter too and figured it was only a matter of time before the other members of our group counseling session would reject her.

When I met Bobbie, I thought she would be a perfect fit for group counseling. She was looking forward to attending and learning how to better manage her emotions along with other women who had similar life experiences as she. During her first group session, Bobbie was open with the others in the group. More open than some in a first session, but not overly talkative. The group went well, or so I thought. The next day Bobbie called and told me she was not coming back.

"I overshared, and they're not going to like me now," she said.

I tried to explore this with her and reassure her that (a) although she had been open in the group, she had not shared too much, and there was no reason for the group to reject her, and (b) she could choose to say less in the next session if she would feel more comfortable with that. But nothing I said comforted her; she was downright embarrassed and feared she would be thought of negatively and cast aside by the group.

While Bobbie did not yet have a deep relationship with any of the women in the group, the life of their relationships was cut drastically short due to her fear of rejection. She was afraid of experiencing more pain in her life. Really, she rejected the group before they even had the chance to reject her!

Fear of rejection often means we don't take chances in our relationships.

Why attempt cooking my husband's favorite meal? He's not going to like it as much as his mama's anyway.

Why bring up my idea in the staff meeting? No one is going to like it anyway, and people will think I'm stupid.

Why go back to the Bible study at church? There's no way the women will like me after I unloaded my horrible past on them.

In other words, why bother if I'm going to be rejected anyway? Instead of fearing rejection, we should fear not having as healthy of a bond with our loved ones as possible. Building that bond can be risky. It means we have to be willing to take a chance. I like this description of how we can fight the fear of rejection:

> If we risk opening our heart to someone who rejects us, it doesn't have to be the end of the world. We can allow ourselves to feel sorrow, loss, fear, loneliness, anger, or whatever feelings arise that are part of our grieving. Just as we grieve and gradually heal when someone close to us dies (often with the support of friends), we can heal when faced with rejection. We can also learn from our experience, which allows us to move forward in a more empowered way.[1]

This outlines a three-prong plan for fighting this fear:

1. Take the risk to open your heart.
2. If you get rejected, feel the emotions that ensue.
3. Ask yourself what you can learn from this experience.

At best, your fear will not be realized, at worst, you can learn from the experience.

The Fear of Abandonment

During my husband's and my long journey toward adoption, I have learned that many children who have been adopted struggle with the fear of abandonment, even if they were adopted as infants. In *The Primal Wound: Understanding the Adopted Child*, Nancy Newton Verrier writes about the impact separation from the birth mother has on the adoptee. While she writes specifically to help those connected with adoption, she notes that the book will "bring understanding and encouragement to anyone who has ever felt abandoned."[2]

You may not have experience with adoption, but you may fear abandonment for other reasons. In their book *Cry of the Soul*, Dan Allender and Tremper Longman III write that "every human relationship is haunted by potential abandonment."[3] Sadly, this fear can sometimes lead to behavior that pushes people away, which is the opposite of what we desire. Remember the issue with communicating "I'm needy"? The fear of abandonment can cause us to send this exact message. Let's take a closer look at where this fear comes from.

The fear of abandonment is often rooted in childhood, when attachment style develops.[4] It's been said that "the answer to why people feel and act the way they do lies in the profound effect of a child's bonding with his or her parents."[5] This theory is related to how an individual physically and emotionally connects with others. It's believed that the way we connect with others begins in childhood, and then carries on into adulthood, impacting all of our relationships. There are four general styles of attachment. Three are insecure (anxious-preoccupied, dismissive-avoidant, and fearful-avoidant) and only one is secure. We'll look at each of these four, with examples to help illustrate insecure and secure attachment. Ultimately, we want to work toward secure attachments in all of our relationships.

Insecure Attachment

People who are not securely attached are said to be either "anxious-preoccupied" or "avoidant." Avoidant attachment style is further broken down into the categories of dismissive and fearful. About 20 percent of people are anxious-preoccupied, while the other 20 percent are avoidant.[6] Those who have *anxious-preoccupied* attachment look to others, in particular their partners, to complete them. Ironically, they try to cling to their loved one while engaging in desperate actions that push their loved one away. Those who are *dismissive-avoidant* emotionally distance themselves from others, while those who are *fearful-avoidant* live in a state of concern over getting too close to people or getting too distant from them. "They see their relationships from the working model that you need to go toward others to get your needs met, but if you get close to others, they will hurt you. . . . these individuals tend to find themselves in rocky or dramatic relationships, with many highs and lows. They often have fears of being abandoned but also struggle with being intimate."[7]

Considering that 40 percent of adults have insecure attachment styles, it's possible some of your relationship struggles stem from an insecure attachment style. If you make comments (or have thoughts) toward your husband such as, "Go ahead and leave—just like my father did," or "What's the use trying? I know we'll wind up divorced. You'll leave me like my dad left my mom," you might be dealing with insecure attachment. Or, perhaps, your insecurity comes out more with friends with thoughts such as, *She hasn't returned my calls or texts in three whole days. I bet I won't ever hear from her again.* Or maybe you fear being abandoned by your children one day so you give in to their every demand. These are all indicators of insecure attachment.

The opposite of insecure attachment is secure attachment.

Secure Attachment

"Securely attached adults tend to be more satisfied in their relationships."[8] Adults who have a secure attachment style were securely attached to their parents as children and successfully became independent from them. With their parents, and then with other people, they are connected, but free. In a relationship they feel safe with the other person, and go to that person when distressed. They feel seen and heard by that person. "Their relationship tends to be honest, open and equal, with both people feeling independent, yet loving toward each other."[9]

If we are secure, we will not live in fear over losing the relationship, even when there is conflict. When we fight with a spouse, we don't automatically assume our spouse will walk out the door and never come back. When we have a disagreement with a friend, we don't assume that's the end of the relationship. When we are secure, we feel freer in our relationships.

While secure attachment typically begins in childhood, it's not too late to work toward becoming more secure in your relationships as an adult. It is possible! However, it may take working with a licensed mental health professional specializing in this area to truly accomplish this task. If you are not sure where to look, I'd like to suggest the American Association of Christian Counselors.[10]

But you don't have to wait to see a counselor to begin fighting this fear: you can fight your fears with the truth of God's Word.

USING THE BIBLE TO FIGHT FEAR

It's been said that the command to "fear not" appears 365 times in the Bible, once for each day of the year. Well, I've got some bad news and some good news about that. The bad news is that this is not true. The Bible does not say "fear not" 365 times. The good news is that when you combine "fear not" with other reminders to not be anxious or to fear God alone, the number is greater than 365![11] If you're struggling with fear of inadequacy, rejection, abandonment—or any other fear that may be impacting your relationships—and want some scriptural reminders to meditate on, read through the following sampling of verses that tell us to have no fear or worry, but to trust in God. You can rest assured that God will never leave you (Deut. 31:6)!

- "When I am afraid, I will put my trust in you." (Ps. 56:3)

- "So do not fear, for I am with you; do not be dismayed, for I am your God. I will strengthen you and help you; I will uphold you with my righteous right hand." (Isa. 41:10)

- "For God has not given us a spirit of fear." (2 Tim. 1:7 NLT)
- "There is no fear in love." (1 John 4:18)

Relationships—especially messy relationships—can be rife with fear. I've only covered three fears in this chapter, but I know you may be experiencing others. Ultimately, all of our fears come from Satan. John 8:44 tells us that Satan is a liar; the father of lies in fact. He tells us we are not good enough. He tells us that we should be and likely will be rejected, abandoned even. This all comes from our adversary, who wants to devour us and ruin our relationships. Remember, 2 Timothy 1:7 says that *God* has not given us fear. It also says that God *has* given us power, love, and a sound mind. Satan doesn't stand a chance against God. He doesn't have a counterargument to love. And love drives out fear.

WORKING ON MYSELF

1. Consider one way that you feel inadequate in a relationship and write about that below.

2. Now, spend some time considering the evidence for the truthfulness of this statement.

3. Have you experienced rejection in any of your relationships? If so, write about that here.

   _____

   _____

   _____

4. What has this experience taught you about being able
   to risk rejection in relationships? *Example: This experience taught me that while rejection is painful, it is not the
   end of the world.*

   ~~_____~~ _____

   _____

   _____

5. Based on the information you have read in this
   chapter on the four attachment styles, which do you
   most closely identify with and why?

   _____

   _____

   _____

6. If you identify yourself as having an insecure attachment style, where do you believe this originates from?
   Write about that below.

   _____

   _____

   _____

7. What Scripture speaks to you the most about fear of
    abandonment? How can you use that verse to reduce
    your fear in relationships?

_____

_____

_____

Dear Lord,

*Please help me let go of my fear of rejection or abandonment.
Help me do the work to become more securely attached to my
loved ones. Please also help me treat other people in a manner
that allows them to securely attach to me. Thank You for how
You love me unconditionally. I know that You will never leave
me, and I pray that as I meditate on this promise, my mind
and heart will seize on to this truth and that it will result in a
decrease in fear.*

In the name of Jesus I pray,

Amen.

8

Surrender Judgment

Hope was depressed. She would shuffle into my office week after week and plop down into the chair. She rarely cried, and once said she didn't have any tears left. Her husband had left her. Followed by their mutual friends. They had chosen him, she said. *If they only knew the whole story*, she often lamented. She had tried to protect him—loving him even after he had been with other women—by not sharing the truth about their divorce. But he got out ahead of her, telling their friends lies and leading them to believe that the split was her fault. Yes, she left him, but only after years of his lies and infidelity. He never admitted to that part, and her friends were gone before she had a chance to share her side of the story.

She says, "The truth is that I didn't even want the divorce. I just needed some space. I had forgiven him before, and I would have forgiven him again. But when he moved another woman into our home, that was it. So, I filed. I get all the blame. And all the judgment that goes along with it."

Hope was on the receiving end of her friends' judgment. I tell her story here because it poignantly illustrates why we need to surrender judgment. For one thing, we never know the whole truth as to why people do what they do. If we did, we would likely be much more understanding. For another, judgment kills relationships.

What do we do with our tendency to pass judgment? Let's start by getting a better handle on the meaning of this loaded term.

BIBLICAL JUDGMENT
VS. WORLDLY JUDGMENT

Judgment. We hear this word all the time. Everywhere you turn, it's there. Facebook statuses. Tweets. Blog posts. It's the battle cry of many.

"Don't judge me."

"Don't judge others."

"You don't have the right to judge."

"Walk a mile in my shoes before you judge me."

"The Bible says not to judge."

It's often used by people when they know they are wrong, but don't want to admit it. Or for the purpose of silencing those who might disagree. The problem is that few people even know what this word really means, and many don't understand the Bible's use of the term.

In Matthew 7:1, Jesus says, "Do not judge, or you too will be judged." Here, Jesus is saying, "Don't judge another person unless you are ready to be judged." He is not saying, "Don't ever have an opinion about something based on your own Christ-centered convictions and values." Clearly, we all do that. We have beliefs about everything from how children should be raised to what we should eat. Yet, oftentimes, what we judge people for doesn't have anything to do with what's right and what's wrong—just differences.

For example, debates abound regarding things like bottle-feeding versus breastfeeding (especially in public). Choice of schooling for children (private, public, or homeschool) is another example. These aren't the types of things we should be judging people on. The purpose of Jesus' directive to "judge not" is that we should not be hypocrites, pointing out the sin of others without recognizing and addressing our own sin. We should always be willing to look into our own hearts and at our own sin. And to do something about it!

So when I say that one of the bad habits we need to break is judgment, I am *not* saying we can't call sin sin or hold others accountable for their sin. Yet, we should not make snap judgments because we don't always know the real situation, as was the case with Hope. We shouldn't decide the verdict and sentence on cases we have no part in. To take the courtroom scenario a bit further, we are not the attorney, the juror, or the judge. Yet, we so often *do* judge, and in a way that is not biblical. As a result, our relationships can become tense, or worse, completely fall apart.

In this chapter, we'll take a look at some of the subtle ways we can judge people, without even realizing it, and then we'll talk about how you can surrender these bad habits and work on building healthier bonds.

Mind Reading

You send a text to your sister. A little "Hey, how are you?" She doesn't reply back instantly like she normally does. An hour turns into a day. You check your phone frequently, and become more worried each time you see she has not responded. You decide your sister is upset with you (or in the hospital). You rack your brain trying to figure out why. You just know that she's wondering why you haven't apologized yet and has decided not to talk with her till you do. So you do. You send a second text, "Hey, is everything okay? I am so sorry for whatever I did to upset you. Will you forgive me? I have been so upset about this since I didn't hear back from you after I texted you yesterday." Your sister instantly replies, "Oh my good-ness! What text? I didn't get one. And I'm not upset with you!" You breathe a sigh of relief. But then a wave of embarrassment washes over you. *I guess that's what I get for trying to read her mind.*

Are any of your relationships suffering because you have as-sumed you knew something about a person or a situation, only to be proven wrong? When we resolve in our mind, even without any evidence, that we know what someone is thinking or feeling about us, it can result in our being upset with that person for no good reason.

I have a confession. After sharing some personal examples in this book, I'm feeling a little nervous about what people will think. *Her relationships aren't perfect. How can she help me?* Did you see what I did there? I instantly went to mind reading! While we should be mindful of the impact we have on other people, and the consequences of our actions, we should not assume the worst in others, or that they will think the worst of us. Instead, we can accept the reality that we do not know what others are thinking unless they communicate their thoughts to us. Instead of wasting time worrying about all the "what ifs" (that ultimately will not help our relationships), we can set aside the notion that we can perform this carnival-style trick.

We can also set aside snap judgments.

Snap Judgments

Imagine you are walking your dog on the sidewalk down your tree-lined street. It's early evening, and there is steady flow of com-muter traffic. You see your friend Sue walking on the sidewalk on the other side of the road. You attempt to catch her eye and wave, but she doesn't acknowledge you. You call out to her, but don't get a reaction. Although cars are whizzing back and forth, you're sure Sue saw you. As she continues walking and your dog pulls on the leash letting you know it's time to go, you continue down the road with your heart pounding and your breath labored, feeling frustrated. Angry. Indignant.

> *What in the world is wrong with Sue?*
> *I can't believe she totally snubbed me!*
> *You know what? I bet she is still upset that I picked out the*
> *cake she wanted to win at the cake walk.*

Your mind starts swirling, and you begin to decide on a reason for Sue's lack of response to you.

But, what if . . .

- Sue was wearing her headphones and didn't hear you calling her name?

- Sue had sunglasses on, at dusk, and couldn't see you through the dim lenses?

- It wasn't Sue at all, but a look-alike—a so-called doppelganger?

You see, sometimes we make a decision about something based on our version of the facts, because we're not willing to wait for the actual facts to come in. We make a snap judgment. In this case, your mind may have told you that Sue was upset with you and ignoring you on purpose, when there are many possible reasons as to why Sue didn't respond. Your snap judgment caused you to feel all kinds of negative emotions, and it could interfere with your relationship with Sue.

When you get home, you pull out the cellphone you left at home and call her. Sue answers "Hello?" to which you reply, "Sue, what's going on? Why didn't you respond to me a little while ago when we passed each other on Maple Drive?"

Surprised at the accusatory tone in your voice, Sue responds,

"I don't know what you're talking about. I've been at home all day with a cold."

Your heart drops. *There I go judging others again. I should have just let it roll off my back. When I called her, I could have asked her politely how she was and if she saw me. I should have known Sue wasn't ignoring me on purpose. Why do I do this?*

You do this—*we* do this—because we have allowed snap judgments to become a bad habit. A friend once shared how she was hurt by a situation that took place at the ministry she volunteered with. Every year the various teams were looked at and rearranged based on volunteers, who came and went. One year, she wasn't asked to serve on a committee she had been a part of for over a decade. As soon as she heard the news, she instantly "knew" that the volunteer coordinator was to blame. *She doesn't like me, and did this to hurt me.*

Feeling deflated, my friend shared her suspicions with a few of the other volunteers. The director of the ministry got wind of it and called her. The director admitted that it was she who had made the decision, not the volunteer coordinator. After she heard the explanation, my friend accepted the decision. But her mind kept returning to how her snap judgment had hurt the relationship she had with the volunteer coordinator, who had been cold toward her at the last volunteer meeting. *Yep*, she thought, *I've done it again. I've got to stop jumping to conclusions.*

Are you in the same position? Finding yourself making snap judgments that damage relationships? Before talking about some solutions, there's one more habit we need to address.

Deciding What's Best for Others

Once upon a time, I was a bit invasive. Blame it on my youth. One of my worst offenses was trying to fix my friends—one friend in particular. Sometimes she asked me for help, and I obliged. But other times I tried to help her, even though she didn't invite my help. Passing judgment on what needed to be fixed in her life and then attempting to force the "solution" resulted in pain for both of us.

I knew my friend struggled significantly with her weight. For the most part, she kept it to herself, but would mention it to me on occasion. I tried to be supportive, and after hearing a radio advertisement one day, I decided I would do more than just be supportive. I called her up and told her about a local gym that was having a special. "Are you interested?" I asked. She replied, "Oh, I don't have the money." *I can solve that problem,* I thought. "How about I pay, as a gift?" I asked. "Yeah, sure. Thank you," she said. I immediately called the gym and paid the fee for the one-month trial membership. I was so proud of myself.

But my plan didn't work out very well. You see, my friend never went to that gym. Money wasn't the only issue. Motivation was another problem. It was frustrating to me that I had wasted my money, and my friend was frustrated too. She later explained she felt I had thrust the gym membership upon her. She didn't know how to say no to my attempts to fix her.

We have to get away from trying to fix people or their circumstances. When we decide for them what they should do, or how they should go about resolving a problem, we are at risk of hurting them and making them angry with us. (Who among us likes it when other people try to "fix" us?) Sometimes trying to help people hurts the relationship. I wonder if we could all just listen to our friends and family tell us the burdens of their hearts without feeling the need to resolve the hurt. If we don't, we're likely to find people shying away from us, or at least shying away from being open with us.

My circle of colleagues and friends includes a lot of helpers— social workers and counselors. I've been on the receiving end of people who love me and just want to make things better for me. I've experienced this in several areas, including our adoption process.

While this journey has been hard for my husband and me, it was also hard for our loved ones who grieved with us and longed to see us become parents. There were times when well-meaning folks offered suggestions. Sometimes my gut reaction was, *Of course we've already thought of that or done that.* I wound up feeling frustrated—and sometimes offended.

Oh, I get it. Like I said, I'm a "fixer" too, even when my counsel isn't being sought. While I need to gently ask the fixers in my life to stop trying to fix me or my circumstances, I also need to take a long hard look in the mirror and figure out if there is anyone *I* am trying to fix. I'm reminded of Matthew 7:5, "First take the plank out of your own eye, and then you will see clearly to remove the speck from your brother's eye."

There's another way that you can work on surrendering judgment. Three ways actually. You can stop, collaborate, and listen.

Stop, Collaborate, Listen

Stop, collaborate, and listen. Okay, okay. Those are the lyrics to a famous (or infamous) song. (If you don't know which one, look it up. You won't regret it.) But more than song lyrics, they are three ways we can surrender judgment. We'll look at each of these, but in a slightly different order from the song lyrics.

Stop

When you are tempted to read someone's mind, make a snap judgment, or "fix" someone, stop your thoughts in their tracks. Ask yourself, "What is the evidence for this being true?" and "What is the evidence against this being true?" Explore all possible solutions before deciding that you know what someone else is thinking about you or how someone is feeling toward you.

After thinking through the answers to these questions, you may land on a more likely explanation than the one you have conjured up for yourself. A former colleague was in my office, when she realized she had misplaced her scheduling book that contained her clients' names and phone numbers. She knew the potential breach of confidentiality and immediately stated, "Don't you judge me for this!" To be honest, I wasn't thinking about my colleague at all. I was thinking about where the book may have gotten off to in order to help her find it. Thankfully, she found it under a book she had placed on top of it in her locked office. But, my coworker could have avoided that snap judgment—and that accusation—had she stopped her thoughts before mind reading, making a snap judgment, and deciding that I was thinking negatively about her for her error.

Listen

Instead of deciding you know what someone else is thinking or feeling about you, ask them. The friend who didn't call you back? Don't mull this over for a week. Give her some time to respond. If she doesn't pick up the phone and call, don't assume she is upset with you. And if she does return your call, don't start the conversation by apologizing for some wrong you imagine you perpetrated. Rather, listen to her. Listen to her tone of voice. If you're still not sure if she is upset with you, check it out by gently asking her rather than accusing her. And then listen to her response. I love the saying "listen to hear rather than to respond." Sit with that for a moment.

[And the next time a friend unburdens herself to you, don't attempt to fix her. Listen. Empathize. Ask what you can do for her. Pray for her! Don't judge what needs to be done and then force it upon her or attempt to do it for her. Just listen.]

Collaborate

Working together in relationships—what a novel concept! (Imagine a winking face emoticon inserted here.) Remember how I said you could ask that friend with a problem what you can do for her instead of forcing your fix on her? You can collaborate with her! (Be careful what you ask for. I asked a boss what I could do to assist with a project, and the response was that I could move to another location and take on the project myself. Um, no thanks.) But, seriously, instead of thinking that the frazzled single mom in your Bible study needs to get it together when she shows up *again* without having done her lesson, offer to take her kids with yours on your weekly trip to the library so she can have some time to study. Instead of looking down on your disorganized coworker, who frequently says she wants you to rub off on her but never seems to take steps to make changes in her life, take some time to help her get organized. Really, collaboration is not rocket science. It simply takes being willing to work together to build a fruitful relationship, rather than one based on judgment.

You can also collaborate with someone in an attempt to repair a relationship broken by judgment. Apologize to each other for the hurt you may have caused. And forgive each other for the offense done to you. Talk about how you want to respond to each other next time one of you is tempted to judge the other (because there is usually a next time).

For example, you can decide that when you and your friend or relative are in a disagreement, you will fight fair. Flip a coin. Whoever wins the coin toss gets to speak first. The winner of the coin toss has ten minutes to share her side of things, then it's the other person's turn. You then both have to remain silent for ten minutes before either of you speaks again, giving you time to think. When fighting, it's important to think about your words and actions. Are you using words that will be helpful to your relationship, or words that will further divide your relationship? The same is true for your tone of voice, volume, word choice, and body language. Are you working toward reconciliation in the relationship or flailing against it? You can collaborate to build a healthier bond.

GOD'S JOB, NOT OURS

As I often do, I decided one evening to take a peek at social media. Of course, that energy vampire took more time and attention than I intended, and I found myself experiencing a wide array of emotions as I scrolled through my newsfeeds. I became disappointed and frustrated with friends who held a different view than I did on the hot-button issue of the day.

Naturally, I began to type out Facebook replies and tweets. I needed to question some folks and set others straight. Typing, editing, and deleting many times. Then the Lord spoke to me and reminded me of James 2:13: "Mercy triumphs over judgment." To give some context, James writes, "Speak and act as those who are going to be judged by the law that gives freedom, because judgment without mercy will be shown to anyone who has not been merciful" (2:12–13). To be sure, there will be a judgment day. But today is not that day, and I am not the judge. I do not have to take on every person I disagree with. Rather, I can be merciful, speaking truth in love as the Holy Spirit leads and not just because I want to or because I think I'm right. I can show mercy rather than judgment. My judgment would not change the positions of the people I love and would only serve to further divide us.

I explained early on in this chapter the difference between a biblical view of judgment and a worldly view of judgment. If we look at judgment as a *sentence* (such as eighteen months in prison for stealing a car), then we know that our eternal judgment can only come from one source: God. We don't have to concern ourselves with "judgment" from others, and we certainly don't have to judge others ourselves.

And speaking of God's judgment, let's close this chapter with a closer look at what Scripture says about this. According to Romans 6:23, the just and fair punishment for our sin is death, and yet the gift of God is eternal life. In other words, we deserve death, but if we repent of our sins and accept God's free give of salvation, we are given life eternally. It's a gift that comes from God, with His eyes wide open. You see, He knows all about us. He knows our every thought and action. He knows our every sin. Yet, He loves us anyway. He loves us so much that while we were still sinners, He sent Christ to die for us (Rom. 5:8). Did you catch that? He *knew* we were sinners, but He died anyway.

You see, God wants us to live forever with Him. There is only one way to God, and that's through Jesus. Romans 10:9 tells us that if we confess with our mouths that Jesus is Lord, and believe in our hearts that God raised Him from the dead, we will be saved. This lifesaving, eternal message is for everyone!

WORKING ON MYSELF

Take some time to see how you might be able to stop, listen, and collaborate in order to surrender judgment in your relationships.

Stop. Think of a time you have "read someone's mind" or made a snap judgment and discovered you were oh so wrong about that person. If you had stopped your thoughts in their tracks, what alternative conclusion might you have arrived at? Share that too.

_____

_____

_____

Listen. Consider who you need to spend more time listening to and less time judging. Write about that below.

_____

_____

_____

Collaborate. How can you collaborate with someone to improve your relationship, to build the healthier bond we've been talking about?

_____

_____

_____

Dear God,

Please help me stop unrighetously judging others. I know it's harmful to my relationships. I want to stop mind reading. I want to start listening more to others. I want to work with people, and not against them. Please help me in all of these areas.

And thank You for sending Your Son to die on the cross for my sins.

In the name of Jesus I pray,

Amen.

Dispel the Past

Jerry and Judy had been married for years before he went to Afghanistan. As war has a way of doing, it changed Jerry. While committed to taking care of his family, when he came back home he was distant from his kids and Judy. The children didn't know anything different; this is how their father always interacted with them. But Judy? Well, she knew (and missed) the old Jerry. The Jerry who swept her off her feet. The Jerry who laughed loudly and enjoyed life. She could cope with the changes, but needed *something,* some indication that she and Jerry would still be close, and that he still cherished her. He did, but had a hard time showing it.

The last straw came for Judy at the wedding anniversary party their Sunday school class had thrown for them. Jerry dreaded the thought, but agreed to the party anyway. It was a total disaster, but the worst part was when someone jokingly said to him, "You may now kiss your bride," and he froze, leaving Judy on the spot too. After a few awkward moments, everyone went back to eating cake and joking around with one another, but the sting never left Judy. She'd had it. That's when they came to me for marriage counseling.

As they shared this experience, Jerry explained that he felt *exposed* in that moment. He'd long struggled with symptoms of post-traumatic stress disorder (PTSD), and being in a crowd always triggered that sensation. But being put on the spot intensified his exposure.

Jerry had emotional wounds that had never healed. As a result, he avoided anything and anyone that might trigger his PTSD, including crowds. He could handle the party as long as he wasn't the center of attention—as long as he kept his back to the wall and his eyes on what was going on around him. But the moment the spotlight shone on him, all bets were off. The past was impacting the present, and his relationship with Judy was at its breaking point.

It is not uncommon for the unhealed wounds of one (or both!) people to be the underlying cause of problems in the marriage. A wife may struggle to be intimate with her husband because lovemaking triggers images of the sexual abuse she experienced as a child. A woman may shut down every time her husband tries to draw closer to her because her first husband was emotionally abusive to her, and she is finding it hard to trust again.

But you don't have to be married to someone to experience relationship problems that are rooted in the past. For instance: the daughter who can't forgive her mother for not stopping her abuser from harming her; the woman who stopped being open with her friends after her former friend broadcast her personal business to the book club; the employee who was once yelled at by her boss in a staff meeting and is now afraid to speak up, even when asked for her opinion.

A traumatic past can absolutely impact how we respond in the present, but we can take away its power—by focusing on the present, focusing on the future, and seeking the face of God.

FOCUSING ON THE PRESENT

One day I was talking with a woman named Dee who told me: "I feel frozen. I don't know what to do next."

Dee went on to talk about her past. Being married to a man

who constantly found fault with her had worn her down and driven her into depression. She recalled how he twisted things around to blame her and how she bought into it. For example, when she would ask him not to leave his coat, tie, and shoes in all different places all over the house after he got home from work, he retorted that it was her problem. If she wasn't such a perfectionist, it wouldn't bother her. He said she needed to get used to things being that way.

His pornography addiction? That was her fault too. After all, she wasn't intimate with him enough. She believed him and berated herself for not being a "good" wife.

Dee told me that after years of this demoralizing treatment, she finally reached out for help. She had hoped going for therapy would fix her problems, that she'd become less of a perfectionist and be a better wife. As her therapy evolved, she learned that while she did have areas that she needed to grow in (we all do), she was not the cause of her husband's behavior. She was encouraged to bring him in for marriage counseling and to her surprise he agreed. After psychological testing, the therapist's suspicions were confirmed: her husband was narcissistic.[1] As Dee started to understand what had been going on for so long, she worked in individual therapy to regain her voice and be more assertive. She learned to take responsibility where she needed to but not allow blame to be unfairly cast upon her. But as she became emotionally healthier, her husband became worse. Then, one day, much to Dee's surprise, he left. When he filed for divorce, she experienced a mixture of sadness and relief.

In the coffee shop that day, her eyes filled with tears as she talked about her past and how it was impacting her present. Not just where men were concerned, but with other loved ones too. Her son was just about grown—graduation day was right around the corner—and she was concerned about their relationship. He had a lot of his father in him and blamed her for his parents' divorce. She knew he was hurt that his dad wasn't around much, but that wasn't her fault. As a result, she and her son frequently butted heads, and she didn't know what to do anymore. Her relationships at church had also suffered. She knew her ex-husband had manipulated their friends, but she was still hurt that none of them had been there for her during the darkest days of her life. Now, she was left looking for a new church.

I wasn't in the counselor role that day; rather, I was in the role of friend, listener, and encourager. What I later shared with Dee is what I'll share with you . . . how to learn from the past but not dwell on it. Here are two tips for not allowing the past to interfere with the present so that you can stay focused on the current relationship:

Choose something positive that reminds you of the truth about the current relationship. For example, Dee chose to wear a locket that had a photo of her and her son from when he was a little boy. The picture where they looked just alike. Whenever she would start to think *he's just like his father* and become upset, she'd open the locket and be reminded that while her son did have some of his father in him and would need to work through that for the sake of his own relationships, he had a lot of her in him too. This thought helped calm her down and restore her loving feelings toward her son in the present.

Remind yourself that the person from the past relationship is not the person in the present relationship. Just because your dad left does not mean your husband will. Just because your first husband abandoned you does not mean your second husband will or that your son will. While Dee's son did act at times like her ex-husband, he was not him. She needed to look at her son for the unique young man he is.

The people in our lives are all unique. It's not fair to thrust upon someone in the present a characteristic of another person from your past. This truth isn't just applicable to new relationships you may be forming, it can also be applied when you want to reset the relationship with a person who has hurt you—but has changed. If this person's behavior has changed, you are not dealing with the same person who hurt you in the past. When it is at all possible, we must give people the opportunity to change and grow. (That's what Dee did. Sadly, her husband did not change, but she had been willing to give him that chance.)

I can't help but think of the apostle Paul. He called himself the worst sinner (see 1 Tim. 1:15). After causing the terrible persecution of Christians, Paul experienced Jesus on the road to Damascus, was converted, and was changed—from the inside out. I love how Ephesians 4:22–24 speaks to us about changing:

> You were taught, with regard to your former way of life,
> to put off your old self, which is being corrupted by its
> deceitful desires; to be made new in the attitude of your
> minds; and to put on the new self, created to be like God
> in true righteousness and holiness.

To be clear, I am not saying that you should stay in an abusive situation, hoping the abuser will change. In you are in an abusive relationship, you definitely need to get to a safe place. **If you are in a domestic violence situation, please call 1-800-799-SAFE.**

However, we should not hold past conflict and discord over someone's head. Enough with the "remember the time you . . ." Remind yourself that the person from the past relationship may not be the person in the present relationship—whether it's literally or figuratively.

FOCUSING ON THE FUTURE

I have a question for you. If you went to sleep tonight, woke up to find a miracle had taken place, and your world is now exactly as you want it to be—all your problems solved—what would be different in your life? What changes would have taken place?

That question, or other variations, is known as the miracle question.[2] I have asked untold numbers of clients this question in an effort to help them create goals, get out of the rut of negatively dwelling on the past, and start thinking about future possibilities. Take a moment to conjure up the most outlandish miracle you think a client shared when asked the miracle question.

Waking up on an exotic island married to a super model? Nope.

Waking up a millionaire, living in a luxurious home? Uh-uh.

Waking up as the president of the United States? Not that either.

You see, the miracles I heard my clients express were not outlandish. At all. Hardly miracles, if you look at a miracle as the bending of the natural order of things. Instead, they were simple. Realistic. Humble things, like . . .

I would know I had received a miracle because my husband would treat me like he did when we were first married.

I would know I had received a miracle because my boss wouldn't be criticizing my work.

I would know I had received a miracle because the sibling I haven't talked to in years would have contacted me.

You see, most people aren't looking for a future filled with fame and fortune, but rather one filled with loving and fulfilling relationships. While we can't control anyone else, we can explore what we want our future relationships to look like and what role we can play in making those desires a reality.

Let me ask you, what would your relationships look like if a miracle were to take place? Think of the miracle as a goal, and start thinking about what it might take to accomplish that goal. Keep in mind that you cannot control other people, but you can control yourself. For example, are you treating your husband as you did when you were first married? Have you had a heart-to-heart conversation with your boss about your work and his criticism of it? Have you tried texting your sister? We can sit around waiting for these so-called miracles, or we can do everything within our power to improve our relationships as we step into the future.

Perhaps you're thinking, *I am in the middle of a tough experience right now. Is there anything I can do to mitigate the damage it could cause in my relationships, both now and in the future?* If so, I have good news for you. When we seek the face of God, tough experiences can actually be used to bring us closer together.

SEEKING THE FACE OF GOD

Sadly, couples that experience a miscarriage are 22 percent more likely to divorce, and couples that experience a stillbirth are 40 percent more likely to divorce.[3] While it's important to offer the reminder that "correlation does not imply causation," these numbers are staggering. I've known couples that are in those statistics. Yet, I've also known many couples that not only survived the loss of a child, but grew closer together because of their experience.

Some shared their stories with me for this chapter and have allowed me to use their own words to describe how their marriages grew stronger after loss. There is no magic bullet presented here.

Only the timeless truth that brings hope and healing: seeking the face of God.

Anne said, "I found it a blessing that our struggles with infertility and miscarriage strengthened our marriage and our relationship with the Lord. I saw a 'down on my knees' kind of brokenness in my husband that I've never witnessed before during our struggle. Our experiences changed him spiritually . . . in a good way!"

Ashley told me that despite suffering seven miscarriages, she and her husband grew closer together. "We just clung to one another. We read devotionals together, we prayed together, we cried together. But we ultimately knew it was all a part of God's plan."

When Kacie delivered a thirty-six-week-old stillborn baby, she and her husband were devastated. I cried reading her story, but was inspired by the way this couple refused to allow their heartbreak to destroy their marriage. She said, "I don't know how people get through this without Jesus."

Dawn and her husband are no stranger to difficult life circumstances. Their ten-year-old son was diagnosed with brain and spinal cord cancer at age two. After all these years of treatment, he is stable, but not in remission. The family has grown stronger despite these challenges. Dawn writes:

> Even when we hurt, even in our struggles, even through the tears, Jesus is still on the throne, and He cries with us and He holds and comforts us. Our faith has grown more through this journey with cancer than it ever would have had we not gone through this. One of our son's favorite verses is Psalm 73:26, "My flesh and my heart may fail, but God is the Rock and firm Strength of my heart and my Portion forever" (AMPC). It's not that we don't have scars, but it is our faith in Jesus Christ that continues to get us through this journey.

My husband and I have also grown closer despite the difficult experiences we have faced. Infertility, failed adoptions, job conflict and employer changes, moves away from home—all of these tough experiences have brought us closer together as we leaned on God and on one another to see us through. We often reflect on God's provision and protection during these times. We thank Him for the way He has orchestrated our lives. We have grown stronger in our faith and in our marriage.

The same is true for Jerry and Judy, the couple whose marriage was in trouble because of Jerry's PTSD. While Jerry was in individual treatment to process the trauma he had endured as a result of being in combat, I worked on helping him and Judy resolve the relationship problems they were having in the present. We couldn't change the past, but we could do something about the here and now—and the future. They were a committed couple, ready to tackle this problem head on.

God gave me the ability to keep my emotions in check as a therapist. It was tough at times, whether due to sadness or joy. The closest I came to having the tears fall was with Jerry and Judy. After one particularly powerful session, as they stood up to leave, Jerry said he was ready to give Judy, his bride, the kiss she had missed out on at their anniversary party. She cried and said she had not felt his touch in a very long time. The emotion almost overcame me. This couple had persisted. They refused to allow the past (both Jerry's military experience and the distance in the marriage) to ruin their relationship. They fought hard and won. As Warren Barfield sings, "Love is not a fight, but it's something worth fighting for."[4] Your relationships are worth fighting for too. And while no relationship will ever be perfect, we can reclaim them to become the relationships that God intended. It's not too late.

WORKING ON MYSELF

1. Ground yourself. No, not *that* kind of grounding!
   Remember in the section on focusing on the present,
   I told you about choosing an object that would remind
   you of something positive in a relationship you're
   struggling in? That's called a grounding technique.
   Take a moment and consider what person you want to
   select, and what object you will select to remind you of
   them. Write that out below.

   _____

   _____

   _____

2. If you went to sleep tonight, and while you slept—a
   miracle took place—and you awoke to find your entire
   world was exactly as you wanted it to be . . . all your
   problems were solved . . . how would you know this
   change had taken place? What would be different in
   your life? How would your relationships be improved?

   _____

   _____

   _____

3. Write out what you can do to help improve one or
   more relationships in your life. Remember, you can't
   control anyone else. So, don't write down what you
   want your husband, children, boss, sisters, brothers,
   friends, or anyone else to do. Write down what *you* can
   do. Go ahead . . .

_____

_____

_____

Dear Jesus,

Thank You for the air in my lungs. Despite anything bad that has happened to me, I am thankful for life. I know You have me alive for a reason. Thank You for my relationships. I pray that I can dispel my past and focus on my present and future relationships. Please help me do everything I can do to reset the relationships You have placed me in.

For it's in Your name I pray,

Amen.

10

Let God

Have you ever wanted to get even with someone? If you spend any amount of time watching *The People's Court*, you'll find plenty of examples of people who do. I recall one episode about a woman who retaliated against another driver after being cut off. It didn't seem as if she was intentionally cut off, but she took it upon herself to try and teach the other driver a lesson. As she started to cut him off in return, she accidentally hit him. He wound up suing her for his damages. Her defense (if you can call it that) was that the other driver should have had better reflexes. But here's the kicker. She said that she was angry with him because her children were with her, and he could have caused an accident by cutting her off! Is anyone else seeing the irony here?

Oftentimes, when people hurt us or do something we don't like, we want to punish them. We want them to "pay" for what they did to us. Sometimes we don't want to wait for due process, and sometimes there's no due process to be had. Regardless, we decide that we'll be the judge and the jury. This can happen the instant we've been wronged (intentionally or not), or it can happen much later as a result of our allowing bitterness to breed in our hearts, leading to the desire to get even.

The defendant and plaintiff in the car accident case didn't know each other, but this chapter isn't about getting even with strangers. It's about the temptation to make people pay for the wrong or perceived wrong done to us—even if the one who hurt us is a friend or relative. Maybe especially in those cases. There is a saying, "Hurt people hurt people." In other words, when we hurt, we tend to hurt other people. But Proverbs 20:22 says, "Do not say, 'I'll pay you back for this wrong!' Wait for the LORD, and he will avenge you." In this chapter, we'll take a closer look at how the desire for revenge can consume us, and how to let God have control rather than taking matters into our own hands.

GETTING EVEN, A BAD IDEA

The desire for vengeance could lead you to do something minor, such as waiting a week to reply to a friend's email because she has not been responsive to you lately and you want her to "know how it feels when you wait for a reply that comes a day late and a dollar short"; or giving your husband the silent treatment today because that's what he did to you yesterday. Or, it could lead you to do something more serious, such as spreading rumors about your ex-boyfriend because he broke up with you, or considering an affair to get even with your husband for cheating on you. It could even be that your desire to get even with someone starts to consume you. That was the case for Lenore.

Lenore sat seething during each counseling session. She couldn't stop thinking about how to get even with her former boss, who was also the owner of the business she worked for. He had known she was having a hard time, but fired her anyway. She sat in shock the day he told her the company was downsizing and that her position had been eliminated and there was no other position for her to move to. Apparently, her two decades of employment with his company had been nothing. To make matters worse, folks who had been at the company for far less time than she still had their jobs. Most of the people laid off were able to retire, but Lenore wasn't ready for that yet. Although she had secured a new position with a different company, the pay and benefits weren't as good, and she hated to start over.

Lenore could think of little else but this situation. "I am so mad I can't see straight. He is going to pay for what he did to me. He deserves what is coming to him." She couldn't sleep and was losing weight due to the worry, leaving her with little appetite. She became obsessed with wanting justice, and it was at the expense of her own emotional health. "Everyone is sick and tired of hearing me talk about it, and they said I need to see a therapist and get over it. Listen, I know I need help, but what I really want help with is getting even with this jerk. Once that's behind me, I'll be back to normal, and I won't stay angry, depressed, and worried. And my family and friends will start liking me again."

Lenore's revenge fantasies weren't helping anyone. She didn't even know how she was going to get even, but she spent plenty of time obsessing over the options. Call the Better Business Bureau and file a report? Tell her ex-boss's wife she'd seen him flirt with his administrative assistant? Lenore needed help with letting go of her desire for revenge and turning the matter over to God. She needed to know—and to trust—God's care for her.

It can be challenging to trust God in the middle of dark and challenging circumstances, but when we study God's Word and see what happens when people put their trust in Him, it builds our faith. If there is a Bible character who had just cause to exact revenge on those who had harmed him, it was Joseph. Yet he didn't, and he flourished as a result. Let's take a closer look at his story as it illustrates how God can take care of us when we trust Him despite the wrongs committed against us.

TRUST THAT GOD CARES

Joseph's father, Jacob, "loved Joseph more than any of his other sons" (Gen. 37:3) because Joseph was born in Jacob's old age and to his beloved wife, Rachel. Because of his great love for Joseph, Jacob made him a coat of many colors. Naturally, Joseph's brothers were jealous and were unkind to him.

Through two different dreams, God revealed His great plans for Joseph, but in an unwise move, Joseph told these dreams to his brothers. Both dreams revealed that one day his brothers would bow down to him, and the second one showed his parents bowing down to him. Joseph's brothers already resented him, and the idea that their little brother would ever be "over" them only added fuel to their fire of hate and antipathy toward him. No one in the family was happy with these dreams, and some of his brothers plotted to kill him.

Thankfully, one brother, Reuben, talked the others out of killing Joseph, but that didn't stop them from throwing him into a cistern. Once Joseph was in the well, his brothers conjured up a plan to make money off him. They sold Joseph to the Ishmaelites, who took him to Egypt. Reuben wasn't around when they did this and was distraught when he discovered Joseph was no longer in the well. In order to cover up their treachery, the brothers dipped Joseph's robe in goat blood and took it to their father to trick him into thinking an animal had killed Joseph. In the meantime, Joseph was sold to Potiphar, the captain of the guard for the Pharaoh in Egypt.

Despite his brothers' plan for him, "the Lord was with Joseph and he prospered" (Gen. 39:3). Yet he did have some trouble. Potiphar's wife wanted to sleep with Joseph, but he refused (good man). This woman wasn't used to not getting what she wanted, and Joseph's refusal likely embarrassed her. Now *she* wanted revenge. She plotted how to get even with him and accused Joseph of having made a pass at her. Potiphar bought the lie and threw Joseph in prison. Genesis 39:21 tells us that the Lord was with Joseph even in prison! As a result, he found favor with the warden and continued to prosper.

I know the story is lengthy, but stick with me because there is such richness here!

While in prison, Joseph correctly interprets the meanings of the dreams of two other prisoners, the king's cupbearer and baker. Two full years later—did you catch that? Two full years! The Pharaoh had a distressing dream and the cupbearer told him about Joseph. Once again, Joseph was able to accurately interpret a dream, a dream that foretold seven years of abundance and seven years of famine that would come to Egypt. After interpreting the dream, Joseph recommended to Pharaoh that he put someone in charge of storing up crops during the time of abundance so that the country would have food during the famine. Pharaoh said to Joseph, "Since God has made all this known to you, there is no one so discerning and wise as you. You shall be in charge of my palace, and all my people are to submit to your orders. Only with respect to the throne will I be greater than you" (Gen. 41:39–40).

Events unfolded exactly as the dream had foretold, and during the years of abundance, Joseph administrated the storing up of grain so that Egypt had plenty of food during the famine. During the famine, food was scarce in Israel, so Jacob sent his sons to Egypt for grain. Genesis 42–47 tells the story of the interaction between Joseph and his brothers. He had the opportunity to get even with them for their attempt to harm him, but he didn't take it. Instead, he said to his brothers:

> Do not be distressed and do not be angry with yourselves for selling me here, because it was to save lives that God sent me ahead of you. . . . God sent me ahead of you to

preserve for you a remnant on earth and to save your
lives by a great deliverance. (Gen. 45:5, 7)

A weeping Joseph went on to kiss every one of his brothers.
We learn in Genesis 47:11 that Joseph "settled his father and his
brothers in Egypt and gave them property in the best part of the
land" in accordance with what the Pharaoh granted. Yes, after the
way his brothers treated him, Joseph not only didn't seek revenge,
he was thrilled to reunite with them and went above and beyond
to take care of them.

When you think about it, Joseph is an Old Testament type of
Jesus. The father (Jacob) was glorified through the son (Joseph),
as God is glorified through Jesus. Joseph loved and forgave people
who didn't deserve his mercy. The same is true of Christ. We need
to trust Him and be more like Him—forgiving and ready to trust
God with the outcome—rather than allowing ourselves to go to a
place desiring revenge.

WHEN TEMPTED TO GET EVEN . . .

Your situation may not be as serious as Joseph's. Or maybe it is
worse. Regardless, "getting even" with others is not the answer to
the problem. When you are tempted to get even, ask yourself these
questions:

1. Will getting even change what happened?

2. Will revenge do further damage to relationships?

3. Will I be putting myself at further risk of harm
   (emotionally, physically, or legally) by trying to punish
   my perpetrator?

4. Will my relationship with God suffer as a
   consequence?

I'm not a mind reader, but I think I can answer these questions for you.

1. No, getting even will not change what happened to you. Nothing can change your past experiences.

2. Yes, exacting revenge will likely harm relationships, either with the person you are exacting revenge on or with those who are negatively impacted by your focus on that agenda.

3. Yes, you very well may be putting yourself at further risk of harm. Perhaps the person physically or sexually abused you. Might that person do it again? Maybe you are planning something that is illegal. Is the person you are angry with worth your incarceration? Even if you are not at risk of physical harm or legal consequences, you will not feel better about yourself or your circumstances by taking justice into your own hands. You will likely experience guilt, shame, and worry. (Do report abuse to the proper authorities—justice is important, but it is different from revenge.)

4. Finally, yes, your relationship with God will absolutely suffer! Justice is God's job, and trying to go around His will is a sin against Him. Anytime we sin, our relationship with Him suffers.

I once had a client who wanted revenge. His neighbor's dog kept digging up his garden and eating his prize-winning produce. He said that although he had a good relationship with the neighbor and had asked him to contain his dog, the neighbor hadn't put a stop to the dog's behavior. So, my client was thinking of putting something in his garden that would make the dog sick. I took him through the above questions, and my client arrived at many of the same conclusions I just shared with you. While making the neighbor's dog sick *might* stop it from getting into the garden, if the neighbor suspected what had happened, he would be upset and may even take my client to court. Ultimately, my client decided not to harm the dog (sigh of relief from counselor). Instead, we talked about other ways he could cope with his thoughts and feelings (while also continuing to address the issue with his neighbor and take other more appropriate actions if necessary).

Even after asking and answering those questions, you might be wondering what to do with the thoughts and feelings you might still be dealing with. Here are three ideas:

1. Write. Journal about your thoughts and feelings.

2. Read. Read Scriptures that remind you of what the Bible says about revenge. (I include some in the "Working on Myself" section at the end of the chapter.)

3. Pray. Ask the Lord to help you overcome this harmful stinkin' thinkin'.

Finally, if you simply cannot get revenge off your mind, please seek the help of a licensed mental health professional.

NOT OUR JOB

It's okay to desire justice. It's even okay to expect and demand justice. In fact, Isaiah 1:17 tells us to *seek* justice. However, the reality is that justice in a fallen world will never be perfect. But God's justice is. Isaiah 30:18 tells us that the Lord is a God of justice, and Isaiah 61:8 says that God loves justice.

In a world filled with so much injustice, it's important to remember that God promises to right the wrongs of this world.

He can certainly use us if we allow ourselves to be used by Him, including for the sake of His justice. But we have to be careful not to take justice into our own hands. It's not our job to do God's job.

I truly believe that if we all "let God" more—striving not to get even, seek revenge, or set other people straight—we'll be happier and our relationships will be healthier.

WORKING ON MYSELF

1. Do you struggle with wanting to get even with others? If so, write about that struggle below. Be as specific as you can with examples of times payback has crossed your mind. How can you be more trusting that God will take care of this for you? How can you let God and let go?

   _____

   _____

   _____

2. Read what God has to say about getting even.

   "It is mine to avenge; I will repay." (Deut. 32:35)

   "Do not say, 'I'll pay you back for this wrong!' Wait for the LORD, and he will avenge you." (Prov. 20:22)

   "Do not say, 'I'll do to them as they have done to me; I'll pay them back for what they did.'" (Prov. 24:29)

   "Do not take revenge, my dear friends, but leave room for God's wrath, for it is written: 'It is mine to avenge;

I will repay,' says the Lord." (Rom. 12:19)

"Make sure that nobody pays back wrong for wrong."
(1 Thess. 5:15)

"Do not repay evil with evil or insult with insult."
(1 Peter 3:9)

Dear Heavenly Father,

You know I have been hurt by others and that I am tempted to get even. Please take that desire away from me and help me not take matters into my own hands, but instead to trust You with the outcome. I pray that I can let You take control of this and all situations of my life.

In the name of Jesus I pray,

Amen.

Be the Bigger Person

T he year was 2004, and my husband and I were spending our first Valentine's Day together as a married couple. Not realizing that February 14 is one of the restaurant industry's busiest nights of the year, we neglected to make reservations for dinner. Unconcerned, we got dressed up and headed out for a night on the town. Dinner would be first. As we drove around the city we kept encountering packed parking lots and wait times that were far too long, and Nick became increasingly hungry and angry—yep, hangry. In a moment of exasperation, my usually calm, patient, and accommodating husband declared, "If we don't find someplace to eat *now*, we are going to Wendy's!" Well, of course, that was not going to do for this young bride of six months. *A fast food restaurant on our first Valentine's Day? I don't think so.* What followed was a very unpleasant conversation—okay, argument—about where we should eat. Thankfully, within a few minutes, we passed by a mom-and-pop Italian restaurant tucked away in a strip mall. My husband pulled in without a word. After parking the car, we walked in silence, and were both relieved to know there was no wait. We were seated immediately, and before the bread basket hit the table Nick broke the ice. His apology led to mine, and we were both quick to forgive each other for the spat that took place during our dinner search. We went on to enjoy a delicious Italian dinner that night and ate at this restaurant frequently until we relocated out of state. We never fail to chuckle over how we almost missed out on a lovely first Valentine's Day because of a silly fuss.

Being the bigger person sometimes means being the first to apologize. It may also mean being the first to forgive. That's a big part of what this chapter is all about: being willing to apologize and being willing to forgive. In this chapter, we'll also take a look at boundaries and talk about the importance of not giving up because of conflicts or challenges.

Being the First to Apologize

Former college roommates Jenny and Jackie had a falling out and wound up not speaking to each other. Here's what led to the rift in the friendship. In an email exchange following a visit, Jenny expressed to Jackie that she didn't think Jackie was acting Christlike as she believed Jackie had been gossiping during their last visit. Jackie retaliated with an unkind reply, expressing her own frustration. If Jenny had been so offended, why hadn't she spoken up during the visit rather than waiting until later to address it? Besides, Jackie thought, Jenny had no room to talk, based on her own history of freely sharing. Of course, Jenny usually poised her gossip as prayer requests. What hurt Jackie the most is that she really had not intended to gossip and didn't think that she was. She was embarrassed and hurt and responded in kind.

While Jackie had served as a bridesmaid in Jenny's wedding, she did not invite Jenny to her own wedding, which took place after the hurtful email exchange. It wasn't that Jackie didn't want Jenny there, but she had not heard from Jenny even after an attempt to reach her, and she was concerned about what it would be like if

Jenny were at the wedding. Would she be distracted by Jenny's presence—as in, wanting to mend this broken fence instead of spending time with other guests? Most importantly, would Jenny's presence distract Jackie from her new husband? In the end, she decided not to invite her former roommate.

Months passed after the wedding, and the first Christmas Jackie and her husband spent as a married couple, she decided to include Jenny in her annual Christmas card mailing. To her surprise, Jenny quickly responded with the humblest letter Jackie had ever received. In the letter, Jenny wrote:

> While I do not deserve your forgiveness, I want to apologize. I never should have sent you that email. Instead, I should have addressed my concern face to face, when we were together. I know I'm not perfect and should have pulled the plank from my own eye before pointing out that speck in yours. Will you forgive me?

Jackie's heart melted, and she immediately forgave Jenny, who quickly replied with an apology of her own, and their friendship resumed. Years later, they still keep in touch and enjoy visits together when they can make them happen.

Jenny was the first one to swallow her pride and apologize for her part in the rift in this friendship. As is often the case when people care about each other, Jackie was soon to follow.

On Choosing Forgiveness . . . and Asking for It

People often mistakenly think that forgiveness is a feeling. It's not; it's actually a choice. We make the decision whether to forgive. When we forgive, we are not saying a wrong done to us is okay, but that the penalty has been paid. There is no more judgment, no more harboring of resentment, no more wanting to get even. When we choose to forgive, we are releasing the wrongdoing so that we no longer carry the heavy burden of holding on to our hurt.

When you are struggling with forgiving someone (or yourself), try starting each day with this reminder: *Today, I am choosing to walk in forgiveness.*

You see, the choice to forgive may just be for today. Tomorrow, you can make the same decision all over again, but don't worry about tomorrow today (Jesus tells us that in Matthew 6:34). Sometimes, forgiveness is a one-day-at-a-time kind of thing.

I have something critically important to tell you: *You can choose to forgive someone even though the person has not said "I'm sorry" to you.* In fact, I would say more often than not, you will not receive the apology you want, maybe even deserve. Sometimes the person who wronged you does not recognize or is not willing to admit what he or she has done. Other times the person is no longer living or has moved away and is no longer in contact with you. Regardless of why the apology never comes, we shouldn't sit around waiting for it. Instead, we can choose to forgive because God forgave us and because His Word commands us to forgive others.

Not only should we choose to forgive those who have hurt us, we also have to ask for forgiveness when we have hurt someone else. Even though we won't always receive the apologies we deserve, that shouldn't stop us from owning up to our own wrongdoings and asking those we have hurt to forgive us.

While apologies are best made face to face (where you can look someone in the eyes and use body language to help convey your message), that's not always feasible. Physical distance, full schedules, or uncertainty about the other person's reaction are a few reasons why it might be better to write your apology. You may apologize through a letter, like Jenny did, or through email. A Skype or phone call is also a good choice when a face-to-face conversation isn't possible.

One final note: it's wise not to tell people that you have forgiven them if they haven't asked for your forgiveness. Doing so can come across as you thinking you are superior, that you are the bigger person! Your statement might trigger them to become defensive. "You're forgiving me? You should be asking me for forgiveness!" There doesn't seem to be any benefit to communicating this message to someone unless he or she has asked for your forgiveness. Just leave that between you and God. (By the way, those you forgive may very well recognize that you have extended grace to them. Your forgiveness could mean more to them than you know, even if they never express it.)

FORGIVING *AND* SETTING BOUNDARIES

While it's important to forgive those who have hurt or wronged you, that doesn't mean you should allow a person to continue doing you wrong. For that reason, it is critical that you set some boundaries with that person so he or she can't keep hurting you. "A boundary shows me where I end and someone else begins."[1] Boundaries help us to establish what our responsibility is and what someone else's is. They prevent other people from trying to take over our lives; and they prevent us from trying to take over the lives of others. They teach us accept responsibility and to hold other people accountable. When it comes to setting a boundary with someone who has hurt you, be clear about the limit you are setting.

For example, you may say,

- "I forgive you, and I ask that you please not call me that name again."

- "I accept your apology, and I trust that you will call me if you are going to be late in the future."

- "I am willing to forgive you and am asking you not to yell at me the next time we argue."

- "Yes, I accept your apology, and in order for our relationship to continue I'm requesting that you communicate with me more promptly."

Notice that in each of these examples, I use the word *and* instead of *but*. If we use the word *but* when we are trying to set protective boundaries, we are "butting out" the first part of the statement. In other words, saying *but* indicates that perhaps we really do not forgive the person. When we use the word *and* after offering forgiveness, we emphasize that both parts of the sentence are true: I forgive you, *and* I will not tolerate this behavior in the future. When we set boundaries with others, we are being the bigger person. Establishing these parameters is a challenge, but important.

A brief section on boundaries can't come close to covering all the important content related to this topic. But I'll be glad to share with you what resource does: the book *Boundaries: When to Say Yes, When to Say No, To Take Control of Your Life* by Christian psychologists Henry Cloud and John Townsend. The book was so popular that it turned into a series with books on boundaries in dating, marriage, kids, teens, and leaders. There's even a book called *Beyond Boundaries: Learning to Trust Again in Relationships.* These are all excellent resources, and I highly recommend them for anyone who struggles with this topic in particular.[2]

BEING THE BIGGER PERSON IN A DIGITAL AGE

I was working with a colleague on a project, and emailed her with a request. She politely replied that she would do her best, but that she did not work from a specific time at night to a specific time in the morning. I was impressed and inspired by her boundary, and let her know that was a great way to set some margin in her life. You see, it's too easy to expect that since we can reach others at any time of the day, that they should have to "jump to it" as soon as we make a request.

Below are three tips for setting boundaries in relationships using technology:

Establish margins. Set some parameters around when you will and when you will not interact with people via technology. Decide when you will stop checking your text messages, emails, or social media accounts. Don't allow the pressure (either internal or external) to force you to give in. Be firm in your parameters. At the same time, accept the margins that other people have established for themselves. Remember, this is not personal. Having healthy boundaries can help ensure healthy relationships.

Think twice before you hit "send." It can be easy to misunderstand a written communication because you do not get to hear the sender's tone of voice or see the person's facial expressions or body language. As a result, you may be tempted to react to a perceived offense in writing, without thinking. As the saying goes, "Write it, regret it." Sending something off without giving it a second thought can lead to relationship problems. It might even be helpful to consider how the tone would be taken if your reply was public (like on your Facebook wall!).

Instead of hastily replying, take some time to reflect on what the person meant, put yourself in his or her shoes, and don't be afraid to ask for clarification. For example, try asking, "Can you help me understand what you mean?" Thinking twice and striving to understand the other person's point of view before you send a message can help with your relationships.

Don't overcommunicate. "Hi, how are you?" "Are you there? Just want to make sure you're okay." "Are you alive?" "If you don't reply in 30 seconds, I'm calling the police!" This may be a suitable series of texts in some rare instances (from a parent to a teenager late for curfew, for example), but in most cases, this is overcommunication. So is sending someone numerous emails, clarifying and re-clarifying a position rather than simply waiting on a response; or, when you are feeling anxious, so is pressing for a response—the "please don't leave me hanging" kind. Overcommunication can damage relationships because it can leave the other person feeling pressured, intruded upon, and annoyed.

Making Up Is Hard to Do

In 1962, Neil Sedaka recorded "Breaking Up Is Hard to Do." It reached number one on the Billboard Hot 100 record chart. Thirteen years later, Sedaka rerecorded a slower version of this song. It also reached number one, this time on the Easy Listening chart.[3] What is it about this song that resonates with so many people? Sedaka's beautiful voice cannot be denied, but I wonder if the real reason this song fared so well is because of the emotional connection that people made with the lyrics.

Sadly, many people do break up. And it's not just romantic couples; people end other types of relationships as well. When the going gets tough, they break up instead of making up. I get it; making up is hard to do. It takes at least one party choosing to be the bigger person. And even if reconciliation does happen, things aren't always the same, but that doesn't mean the relationship has to end. It's like when a child grows up and moves away from home. The parent-child relationship changes, but it doesn't end. It's just different.

The truth is, just because something isn't perfect doesn't mean we have to throw it away. The following story illustrates what we often do in relationships—and what we can do instead.

One beautiful May, Nick and I were in Italy (thanks to the United States Navy). While there, I went in to the Navy Exchange (NEX) and found a beautiful yellow top. It was made by one of my favorite designers and was my absolute favorite color. I had to have it. I carefully tucked it in my suitcase for the long flight home. After wearing it for the first time, I noticed a couple of imperfections around the pocket of the blouse. Since I could not return it to the NEX, I contacted the company, who agreed to exchange it for me. I sent in that imperfect canary-colored top and waited for a perfect one to return. It never came. The company contacted me and explained that they were mistaken about having any more of this particular style and color in stock. So, in exchange for my beloved blouse, I received a gift card.

I could have kept the yellow blouse despite the flaw, but because it wasn't perfect, I cast it aside (that still makes me sad!). It's easy to do the same in our relationships. Rather than being accepting of the minor flaws (or even the major ones), acting like grown-ups and apologizing and forgiving, we often give up. We separate from our spouse. We stop calling our cousins. We miss out on time with our mother. We forgo our friendships.

But let me ask you, would you rather lose out on the relationship altogether or accept it for what it is after a conflict or change? In Romans 12:18 Paul says, "If it is possible, as far as it depends on you, live at peace with everyone."

A friend of mine shared with me some of her story, which involved forgiveness, healing, and reconciliation. Speaking of herself, her ex-husband, his wife, and her current husband, she said, "In the past, the four of us have been cordial at best. We were never really on the same page about many things until we were all part of a counseling experience that has radically changed our lives and the status of our relationships forever. We now have restoration that has all been washed over by the grace and love that only the Lord could provide."

She explained that after a great deal of work in therapy that integrated their Christian faith, the four of them were able to work through some significant issues related to one of their children. The catalyst for this change was the forgiveness that the former spouses extended to one another. Each of them made a decision to "be the bigger person" for the sake of their child. Forgiveness was the only path they had toward reconciliation.[4]

Sadly, reconciliation is not always possible. On occasion, being the bigger person means recognizing when you've done everything you can do, such as when the friend or family member refuses to respond to your efforts to reconcile. When you want to mend a relationship, it can be difficult to accept when the other person doesn't want to do the same. Sometimes relationships cannot be repaired because the other person is not willing to reconcile—or because resuming the relationship would not be safe. Yet, you don't have to lose hope. John Bunyan reportedly said, "You can do more than pray after you have prayed, but you cannot do more than pray until you have prayed."[5] So, start with prayer and then see how God leads you to respond.

Lots More Valentine's Days

Since 2004, Nick and I have enjoyed many more Valentine's Days together. Not all of them have been as picture perfect as a Hallmark greeting card, but they are all treasured memories because of the love we have shared in good times and in bad. A big part of our relationship has been learning to say "I'm sorry"—a lot. And forgiving one another even more. The forgiveness and grace we are able to offer each other does not come from our own strength. If that's what I relied on, I might still be upset that my husband wanted to take me to a fast food restaurant for our first Valentine's Day!

No, instead, our strength to apologize and forgive comes from the Lord. I love what Daniel 9:9 tells us: "The Lord our God is merciful and forgiving, even though we have rebelled against him." And because of the forgiveness that I'm offered even when I oppose God, I am able to forgive Nick when we are in opposition, and he so graciously forgives me as well.

The most famous line from Erich Segal's novel *Love Story* is, "Love means never having to say you're sorry." I completely disagree. If we love someone, we should be willing to ask for forgiveness when we've done something wrong. And we should forgive others as God has forgiven us (Col. 3:13). This is what being the bigger person is really all about.

WORKING ON MYSELF

1. I want to challenge you to think hard and answer honestly. Do you need to apologize to someone? If so, write down the name(s) and what you will say to apologize.

   _____

   _____

   _____

2. Now, do you need to forgive someone? Maybe that person has apologized, maybe not. That part doesn't matter. Take some time writing about who you need to forgive, and why. Select a Bible verse about forgiveness that you can reflect on as you choose daily to walk in forgiveness. I'll include some below to get you thinking in that direction.

   • "If you hold anything against anyone, forgive them." (Mark 11:25)

   • "Be kind and compassionate to one another, forgiving each other, just as in Christ God forgave you." (Eph. 4:32)

   • "Bear with each other and forgive one another if any of you has a grievance against someone. Forgive as the Lord forgave you." (Col. 3:13)

   _____

   _____

   _____

Dear Lord,

Thank You for Your merciful gift of forgiveness. Please help me extend that same grace to other people. Help me apologize freely and forgive with abandon. If I need to establish boundaries or respect boundaries, guide me in how to do that. Help me be the bigger person in my relationships.

Amen!

12

Relational Reset

O f all our relationships, our relationship with God, who loves us unconditionally, is the most important. We are His creation, and He longs for us to see ourselves and others the way that He sees us. It's only because of our relationship with Him that we can accept ourselves or anyone else as His beloved creation.

In *Giddy Up, Eunice: Because Women Need Each Other*, Sophie Hudson (aka "Boo Mama") writes about three sets of women from the Bible: Mary, the mother of Jesus, and Elizabeth, the mother of John; Ruth and her mother-in-law, Naomi; and Lois and Eunice, the grandmother and mother of Timothy (a protégé of Paul). Hudson is right: women do need one another. My church recently studied Ruth and Naomi during a Wednesday night Bible study. The pastor pointed out that not only did Ruth and Naomi depend on each other for their very survival, but they both relied on Boaz. They needed that relationship for financial and physical security in life.

Yes, women need men too. We need our fathers, our brothers, our husbands, our sons. We need our bosses, colleagues, neighbors, Sunday school teachers, and pastors. People need one another. We were not designed to walk through this life alone. Hebrews 10:25 tells us to not give up meeting together. You know the expression

"When the going gets tough, the tough get going." It's true, relationships are tough and will always be tough, but with God's help, we can reset them to be what God intended them to be. We need to unlearn the habit of unacceptance in order to improve them.

THE IMPORTANCE OF ACCEPTANCE

Have you ever thought, *There's no way he would like me*, or, *She's too well-liked to want to be friends with me*? Sometimes you're right; maybe you're *not* that person's type, and perhaps the other person is not interested in being your friend. Could it be the problem is that you don't accept yourself? That you are self-sabotaging, that you've decided you're not worthy of the love or attention from a particular person? If you are not able to accept yourself, it will make it more difficult for others to accept you—and for you to accept others. Do you define yourself by worldly standards (educational level, marital status, success, income?), or have you accepted the truth that you are complete in Christ? This doesn't mean that you stop striving for God's best in your life, nor does this mean you stop striving to be more like Christ. But it does mean you stop playing the comparison game. It means you stop pining for what other people have and focus on what God has. It means you recognize that you are and have everything you need as a beloved child of the King. When you realize this, you are able to genuinely accept other people and can be okay when others don't accept you.

It's not enough to just set realistic expectations of others; you have to learn to accept people as they are. This gets tricky. I'm not advocating that you support someone's bad behavior, and I'm certainly not suggesting that people can't change. At the same time, relationships will never flourish if you keep trying to change the other people in your life.

Are you ready and willing to accept that you and your sister don't have a lot of the same interests? Instead of trying to force her to change, or being frustrated that you have nothing in common, try intentionally finding something the two of you can relate on. The same hometown sports team you can cheer on together or a television program you can watch while texting back and forth about, perhaps?

Are you ready and willing to accept that your husband thinks more concretely than you would like? Instead of being coy with him, try telling him directly what you'd like for that next special occasion instead of being frustrated when he doesn't get the birthday, holiday, or anniversary hint.

Are you ready and willing to accept that your friend doesn't like talking on the phone? Instead of feeling annoyed with her, try working on a compromise as to what you will text/email about and what you will wait to chat about in your next face to face visit.

You will stay exhausted and frustrated as long as you try to change others. There comes a time when we have to ask ourselves an important question: Can I accept this person even if he or she does not change? Sometimes the answer has to be *no*. Many times, we can accept the person *if* we choose to. My husband and I have done this on more than one occasion in our marriage.

He was on active duty military when we tied the knot. A couple of weeks after our wedding, we moved two states away from my hometown, and I started graduate school and took a part-time job at a retail store. One Saturday on my lunch break, I drove across the street from the mall where I worked to our apartment. I told Nick that I didn't feel well and was thinking of not returning to work. "I'm going to call my boss." He stopped me. "What do you mean you're not going back to work today?" he asked. I replied, "Like I said, I don't feel well." He responded, "I'm sorry you don't feel well. Can I get you some medicine? That way you can feel better and go back to work."

Now, before you think my husband was just trying to get rid of me in order to have the house to himself to watch the big game in private, that wasn't the case. Remember how we talked about expectations in an earlier chapter? That's what this came down to. Being in the military, Nick didn't "call in sick" ever. And I mean *ever.* He had the same expectation for me that he had for himself—don't ever call in sick unless (or maybe even if) you are on your deathbed. That wasn't me. That wasn't ever going to be me. (Besides, all the research shows you should not go to work when you are sick. So, there is your doctor's excuse. You're welcome.)

Nick and I had a "chat" about my decision not to return to work that day. He did come around to understanding my point of view and sweetly tucked me into bed with some ginger ale on my bedside table. But, first, he had to accept that we weren't going to see eye-to-eye on this. He had to accept that I wasn't going to live my life exactly like he lives his. Our values and perspective in this particular area were different. His military background taught him one thing, and my lived experiences taught me another. (Not for nothing; he came around more wholeheartedly to my side of things once he was no longer active duty!) Sometimes we simply have to accept the other person in order for our relationship to remain healthy. And this comes back to love.

IT ALL COMES BACK TO LOVE

Matthew 22 records this passage between a lawyer and Jesus:

> "Teacher, which is the greatest commandment in the Law?"
> Jesus replied: "Love the Lord your God with all your heart and with all your soul and with all your mind. This is the first and greatest commandment. And the second is like it: Love your neighbor as yourself. All the Law and the Prophets hang on these two commandments." (Matt. 22:36–40)

Let's break this down to one sentence: *Everything comes down to love.* We are commanded—not asked or pleaded with—but commanded to love God and people. How we love others impacts them deeply.

Are you familiar with the book of Job? In this beautiful book of the Bible, Satan insists that Job would curse God if He removed His hand from Job's life. God knew that wasn't the case and allowed Satan to cause serious pain and sorrow in Job's life. He lost everything, y'all. Job had four friends who came to him to offer their views as to why he was suffering. Three of them offered no support whatsoever. In fact, in Job 16:2, he calls them "miserable comforters."

Does this expression prick your heart? Have you ever had a so-called friend kick you when you were down? I'm not talking about speaking truth in love when it's needed; rather, I'm talking about the likes of Job's friends who blamed him for his sorrow and insisted his sin was the cause. Worse yet—have you *been* this miserable comforter? There's an expression that says in order to have a friend, you have to be a friend. How you treat your friends and all of your loved ones most certainly impacts the relationship you have with them. Don't be a miserable comforter. Instead, try to understand the reason they are in the position they are in. Be empathetic, listen to understand (rather than thinking about what you are going to say next), and love them. It is the second of only two commands. Everything else hangs on it. Jesus said so.

As you close this book, remember this: We can reset our relationships to be the way God intended them to be: with Him at the center, loving others as we love ourselves. When we do these things, God is glorified.

In the days ahead, I pray you'll be ready to tackle the issues—and the habits—that have been holding you back in your relationships.

That you have learned ways to break bad habits and build

healthier bonds and will take the brave step to silence insecurity and deal with disappointment.

That you'll work to overcome offenses and talk straight.

That you'll kick envy to the curb and forget all about your fear.

That you'll let go of the things in your past that are harming your relationships today.

That you'll be able to surrender judgment, dismiss blame, and take responsibility for yourself.

That you'll be able to apologize, forgive readily, and leave payback to God.

It's time. It's time we reset our relationships.

Dear Lord,

My earthly relationships are with other human beings, and none of us are perfect. I know they will be a struggle, but I am seeing You can redeem my relationships. Together we can reset the ones that are not healthy so that they can look a lot more like what You intended. I pray for those I am in relationship with—that they will know how much I love them and even more how much You love them. I pray that You will get the glory in my life and through my relationships.

In the name of Jesus I pray,

Amen!

Helpful Resources

Dan Allender and Tremper Longman III, *Cry of the Soul: How Our Emotions Reveal Our Deepest Questions About God* (Colorado Springs: NavPress Publishing, 1994).

Gary Chapman, *The 5 Love Languages: The Secret to Love That Lasts* (Chicago: Northfield Publishing, 2015).

Tim Clinton and Gary Sibcy, *Attachments: Why You Love, Feel, and Act the Way You Do* (Grand Rapids: Thomas Nelson, 2009).

Henry Cloud and John Townsend, *Boundaries: When to Say Yes, When to Say No, To Take Control of Your Life* (Grand Rapids: Zondervan, 1992).

Francis Chan and Lisa Chan, *You and Me Forever: Marriage in Light of Eternity* (San Francisco: Claire Love Publishing, 2014).

Max Lucado, *Fearless: Imagine Your Life without Fear* (Nashville: Thomas Nelson, 2009).

Alex Kendrick and Stephen Kendrick, *The Love Dare* (Nashville: B & H Publishing Group, 2008).

Beth Moore, *So Long, Insecurity: You've Been a Bad Friend to Us* (Carol Stream, IL: Tyndale, 2010).

Acknowledgments

I'd like to offer a heartfelt thank-you to Moody Publishers and the entire team for their incredible work on this manuscript. A hearty thank-you also goes out to Liz Heaney. You pulled more out of me than I thought I had to give. I'm grateful.

To my agent, Diana Flegal, with Hartline Literary Agency: Thank you! I'm so grateful for your kindness, encouragement, and wisdom.

To my dear friends—I love you all! Whether we met through school, work, or community, you are such an important part of my life. Thanks so much for your support. I'd also like to thank everyone who takes the time to read the words God has guided me to write. I write for you!

Being on faculty at Liberty University is an honor and blessing. I would be hard-pressed to find a finer group of people to work with than my esteemed colleagues and bosses. But my work would be meaningless without the students—past, current, and present. Y'all make coming to work meaningful and enjoyable!

I'd also like to recognize my home church of over thirty years. Northgate Baptist, and the current and former members and staff, has played a tremendous role in my life. To my pastor, Dr. Barry Jimmerson, and his wife, Tina: We are so blessed by you both. Northgate peeps—I love you all.

To my precious family: I sure was blessed to be placed into the Stephens and Shaler/Toogood clans! My parents are the best there ever was, and I've been doubly blessed because I have amazing parents-in-law too (and they sure did raise an awesome son—my husband, Nick!). Three sisters, a brother, two nephews, two brothers-in-law, and lots of aunts, uncles, and cousins—I've learned a lot about relationships from being in them with each of you! And to my precious AJ: The very thought of you brings tears to my eyes. The love I have for you may very well cause my heart to burst.

To my Lord and Savior Jesus Christ, thank You for Your grace and mercy. I pray the words of this book, and their impact, bring glory to our Father.

Notes

Chapter 1: Silence Insecurity

1. Beth Moore, *So Long, Insecurity: You've Been a Bad Friend to Us* (Carol Stream, IL: Tyndale House Publishers Inc., 2010).
2. Stephanie Castillo, "Body Image Survey Shows Social Media Marketing Making Women More Insecure," *Glamour*, 2014, http://www.medicaldaily .com/glamour-body-image-survey-shows-social-media-making-women-more-insecure-307599.
3. Dictionary.com Unabridged, based on the Random House Unabridged Dictionary, © Random House, Inc. 2018, s.v. "self-worth," http://www .dictionary.com/browse/self-worth.

Chapter 4: Talk Straight

1. Berit Brogaard, "5 Signs That You're Dealing with a Passive-Aggressive Person," *Psychology Today*, November 13, 2016, https://www.psychology today.com/us/blog/the-superhuman-mind/201611/5-signs-youre-dealing-passive-aggressive-person.
2. Amanda Greene, "7 Things You Didn't Know about Your Taste Buds," *Woman's Day*, July 18, 2011, http://www.womansday.com/health-fitness/ wellness/a5789/7-things-you-didnt-know-about-your-taste-buds-119709.

Chapter 5: Dismiss Blame

1. Henry Cloud and John Townsend, *Boundaries: When to Say Yes, When to Say No, To Take Control of Your Life* (Grand Rapids: Zondervan, 1992), 250.
2. Ibid.
3. Ibid.

Chapter 6: Eradicate Envy

1. Genesis 4.
2. Jonathan Kravetz, *How to Deal with Jealousy* (New York: PowerKids, 2007), 5.
3. Dan B. Allender and Tremper Longman III, *Cry of the Soul: How Our Emotions Reveal Our Deepest Questions about God* (Colorado Springs: NavPress Publishing Group, 1994), 47.
4. Ibid., 47.
5. Robert Emmons, *Thanks!: How the Science of Gratitude Can Make You Happier* (New York: Houghton Mifflin Company, 2007).

6. Ibid., 30.
7. Ibid., 44.
8. Ibid., 99.
9. "What's Hebrew for Repent?," Grace Thru Faith, April 10, 2009, https://gracethrufaith.com/ask-a-bible-teacher/whats-hebrew-for-repent.
10. "What Does Repent Mean?," Grace Thru Faith, July 13, 2016, https://gracethrufaith.com/ask-a-bible-teacher/what-does-repent-mean.

Chapter 7: Forget Fear

1. John Amodeo, "Deconstructing the Fear Rejection," *Psychology Today*, April 4, 2014, https://www.psychologytoday.com/us/blog/intimacy-path-toward-spirituality/201404/deconstructing-the-fear-rejection.
2. Nancy Newton Verrier, *The Primal Wound: Understanding the Adopted Child* (Baltimore: Gateway Press, 1993), back cover.
3. Dan B. Allender and Tremper Longman III, *Cry of the Soul: How Our Emotions Reveal Our Deepest Questions about God* (Colorado Springs: NavPress Publishing Group, 1994), 110.
4. Attachment theory is credited to Dr. John Bowlby, with later significant contributions offered by Dr. Mary Ainsworth.
5. Tim Clinton and Gary Sibcy, *Attachments: Why You Love, Feel, and Act the Way You Do* (Grand Rapids: Thomas Nelson, 2009), back cover.
6. Lisa Firestone, "How Your Attachment Style Impacts Your Relationship," *Psychology Today*, July 30, 2013, https://www.psychologytoday.com/blog/compassion-matters/201307/how-your-attachment-style-impacts-your-relationship.
7. Ibid.
8. Ibid.
9. Ibid.
10. To find a counselor through Christian Care Connect, visit https://connect.aacc.net.
11. John Gaultiere, "Fear Not . . . 365 Days a Year," Christian Broadcasting Network, October 21, 2011, http://www1.cbn.com/soultransformation/archive/2011/10/21/fear-not.-365-days-a-year.

Chapter 9: Dispel the Past

1. "Narcissism is often interpreted in popular culture as a person who's in love with him or herself. It is more accurate to characterize the pathological narcissist as someone who's in love with *an idealized self-image*, which they project in order to avoid feeling (and being seen as) the real, disenfranchised, wounded self. Deep down, most pathological narcissists feel like the 'ugly duckling,' even if they painfully don't want to admit it." This definition is found at www.psychologytoday.com/blog/communication-success/201409/10-signs-youre-in-relationship-narcissist.
2. This is a foundational question in Solution-Focused Brief Therapy, which "concentrates on finding solutions in the present time and exploring one's

hope for the future to find quicker resolution of one's problems." See "Solution-Focused Brief Therapy," https://www.psychologytoday.com/us/therapy-types/solution-focused-brief-therapy.

3. Amanda Gardner, "Couples at greater risk of breakup after pregnancy loss," CNN, April 5, 2010, http://www.cnn.com/2010/HEALTH/04/02/breakup .miscarriage.pregnancy/index.html.

4. Warren Barfield, "Love Is Not a Fight" (lyrics), ©2008 Provident Label Group, LLC.

Chapter 11: Be the Bigger Person

1. Henry Cloud and John Townsend, *Boundaries* (Grand Rapids: Zondervan, 1992), 31.

2. Another excellent resource for those struggling with setting boundaries in relationships: http://www.boundariesbooks.com.

3. Wikipedia, s.v., "Breaking Up Is Hard to Do," last edited November 20, 2018, https://en.wikipedia.org/wiki/Breaking_Up_Is_Hard_to_Do.

4. It may be that you are also in a relationship that needs professional help. If so, I encourage you to seek help from a Christian counselor. To find a counselor through Christian Care Connect, visit https://connect.aacc.net.

5. Quote from John Bunyan, *The Westminster Collection of Christian Quotations,* compiled by Martin H. Manser (Louisville: Westminster John Knox Press, 2001), 294.

DISCOVER WHY WORDS MATTER IN A NOISY WORLD

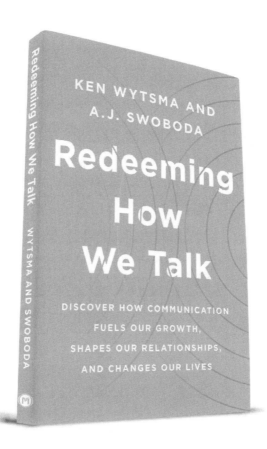

Imagine how Christians could spark change in their families, churches, and communities if they learned to use words like Jesus did. By exploring what the Bible has to say about conversation and the importance of words, *Redeeming How We Talk* teaches us the nature, purpose, and practice of godly speech.

978-0-8024-1617-9 | also available as an eBook